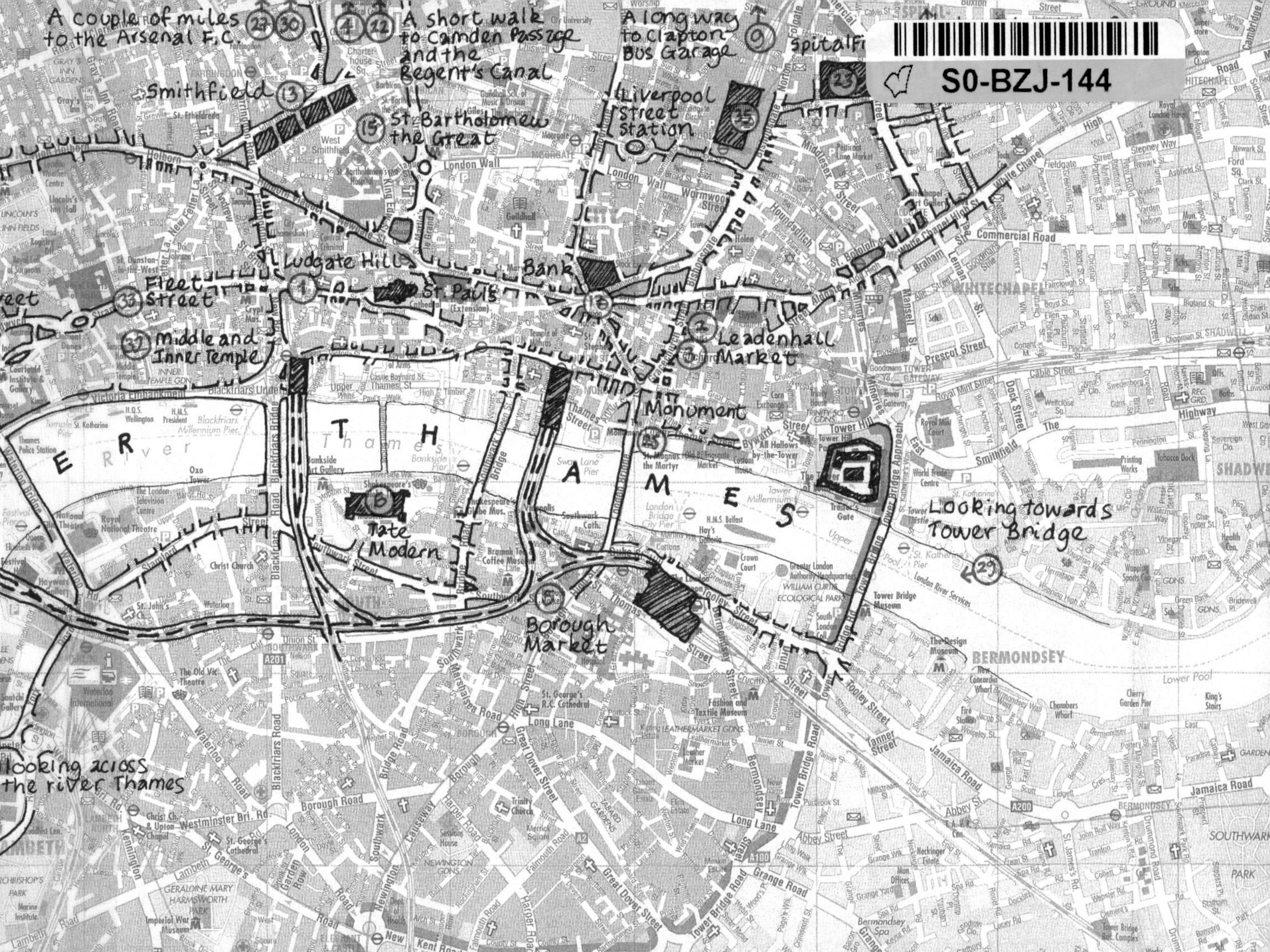

A couple of miles to the Arsenal F.C.
27 30
4 12
A short walk to Camden Passage and the Regent's Canal
A long way to Clapton Bus Garage
9
Smithfield
13
St Bartholomew the Great
15
Liverpool Street Station
35
23
Ludgate Hill
1
St. Paul's
Bank
16
Fleet Street
33
Middle and Inner Temple
32
Leadenhall Market
2
3
Monument
25
T H
E R
A M E S
Tate Modern
Borough Market
Looking towards Tower Bridge
29
looking across the river Thames

LONDON IN LANDSCAPE

CONTENTS

LONDON IN LANDSCAPE

Karen Neale

London memories
Karen Neale

Methuen

1 3 5 7 9 10 8 6 4 2

First published in Great Britain in 2006 by Methuen

Methuen & Co Ltd
11–12 Buckingham Gate
London SW1E 6LB

The endpapers are in the style of a map of London published by Geographic Publishers GmbH, Munich, Germany
which the author acknowledges with thanks.

ISBN 10: 0 413 77619 0
ISBN 13: 978 0 413 77619 8

A CIP catalogue record for this book is available from the British Library

Designed by Bryony Newhouse

Printed in Great Britain by Bath Press

FOREWORD

by The Lady Soames, LG, DBE

I am very happy to have been asked to write the foreword to this delightful collection of sketches by Karen Neale of London scenes. I have had the pleasure of knowing Karen ever since 2001, in which year she was awarded a Travelling Fellowship by the Winston Churchill Memorial Trust of which I was then Chairman of Trustees. The fellowship took her far afield to World Heritage cities and other far flung exotic places, but on her return she took up again the project upon which she had just started when she received the Fellowship – that of sketching London scenes – and this collection is the result of several years' dedicated work.

Karen has her own most pleasing style, and she conveys her characteristic way of looking at her subject – and uniquely, I think – tells her audience in the notes she writes around the edges of her drawings her thoughts and observations as she sketches and paints. It is fascinating to be able to see views of London through her eyes, and for myself, I have frequently found she has opened up a new dimension of a familiar scene, as well as introducing me to new ones.

I hope indeed that Karen will ever heed her art teacher's precept to 'always keep a sketchbook on you', and always have her biro and field box of watercolours to hand, so that we may continue to enjoy her natural and fresh view of many scenes – but especially, as in this book – of those which it is so easy to take for granted.

Mary Soames
London, September 2006

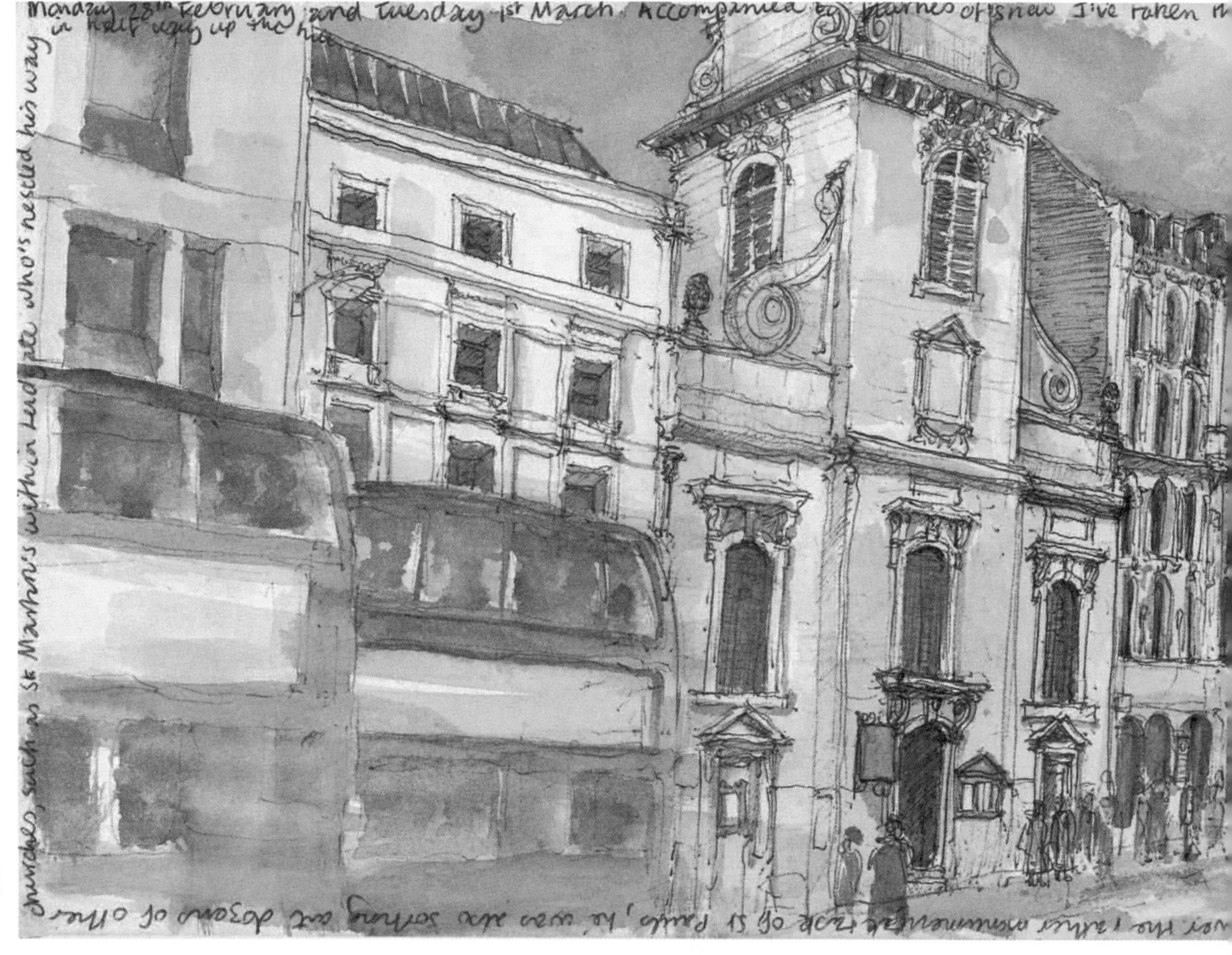
Monday 28th February and Tuesday 1st March. Accompanied by flurries of snow I've taken

1

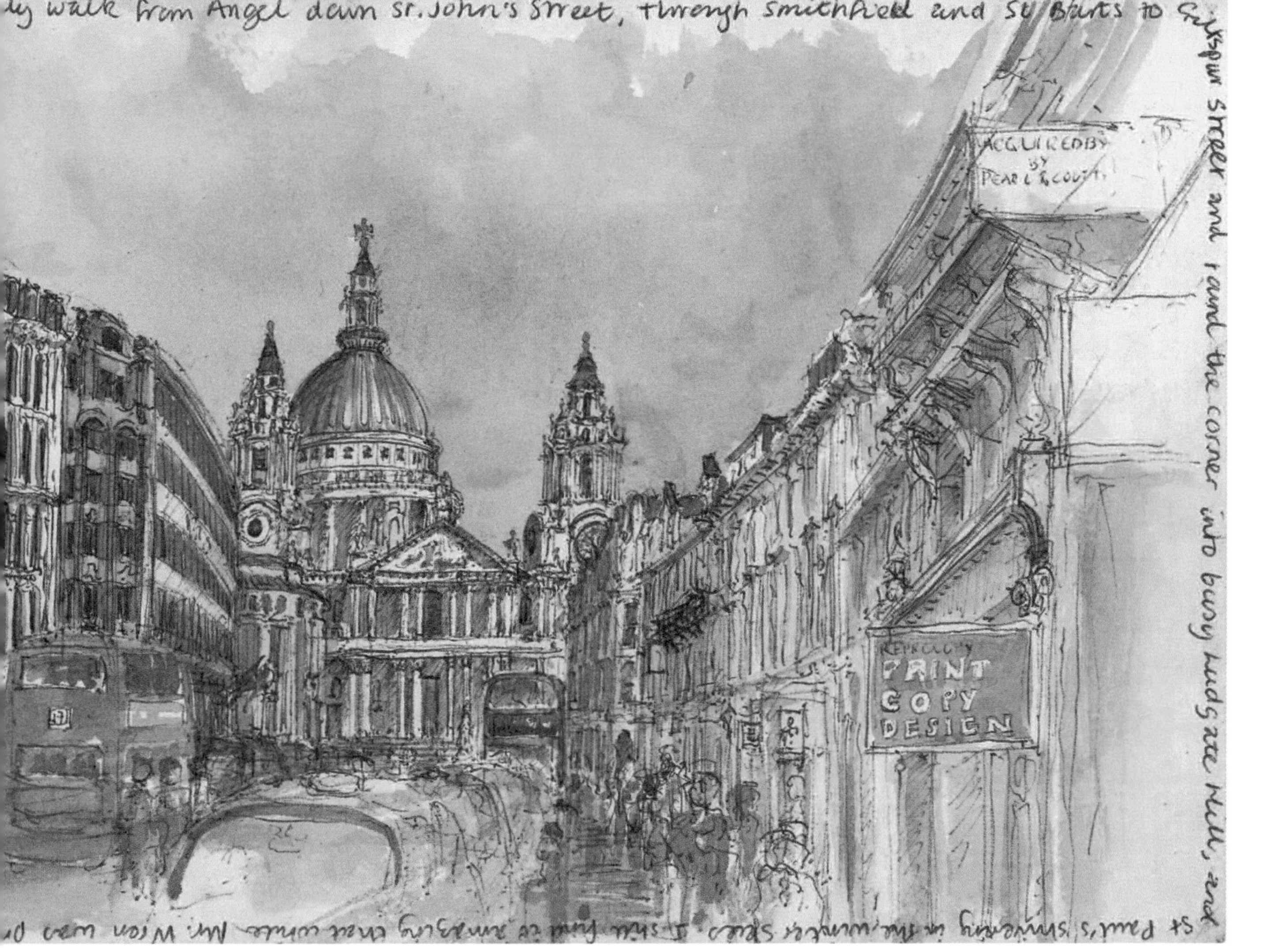
walk from Angel down St. John's Street, through Smithfield and St Barts to
spur Street and round the corner into busy Ludgate Hill, and
St Paul's shivering in the winter sleet. I still find it amazing that while Mr. Wren was
ACQUIRED BY
BY
PEARL & COUTTS
PRINT
COPY
DESIGN

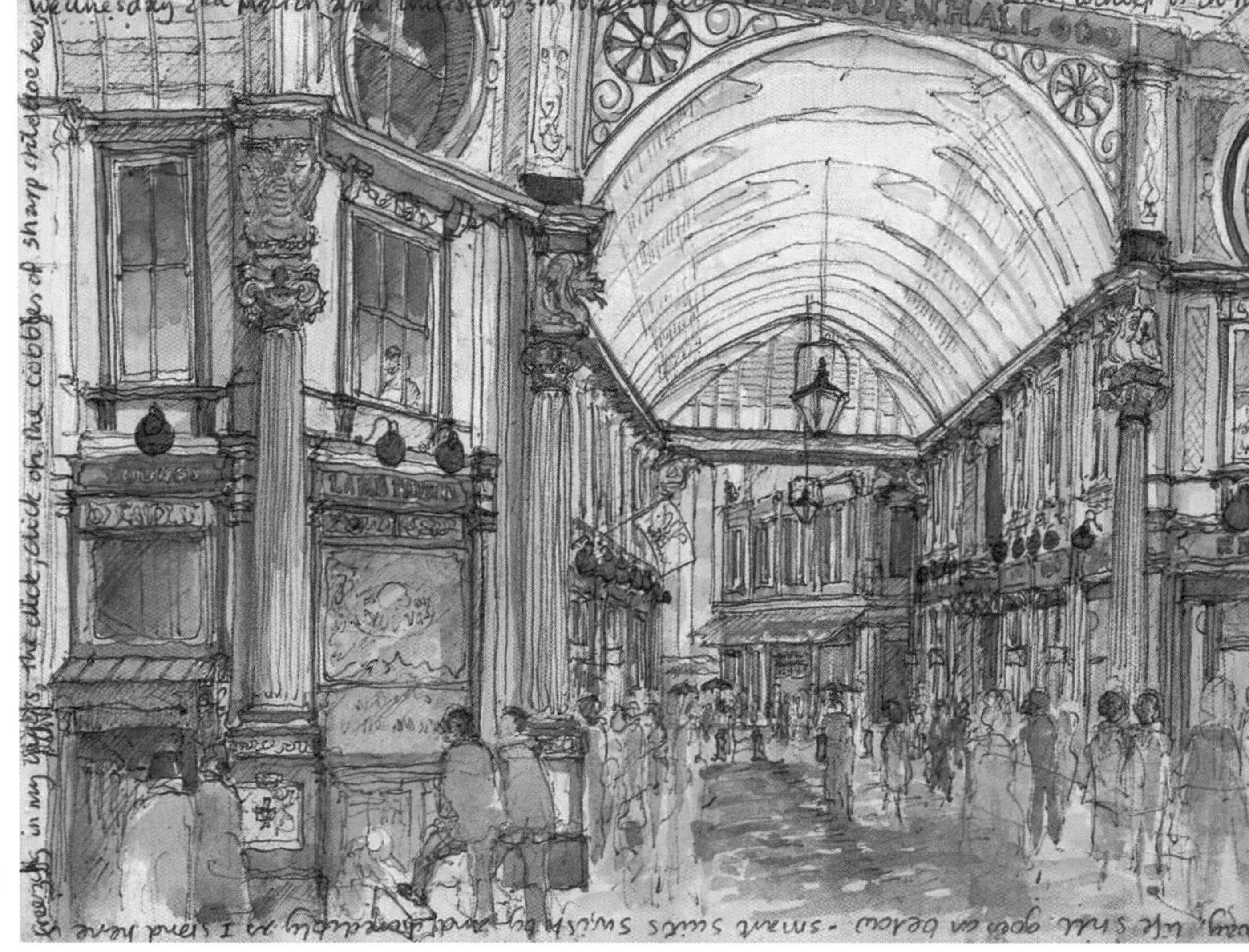
Wednesday 2nd March and Thursday 3rd March
LEADENHALL
well, winter is in
the click, click on the cobbles of sharp
life still goes on below - smart suits swish by
as I stand here

2

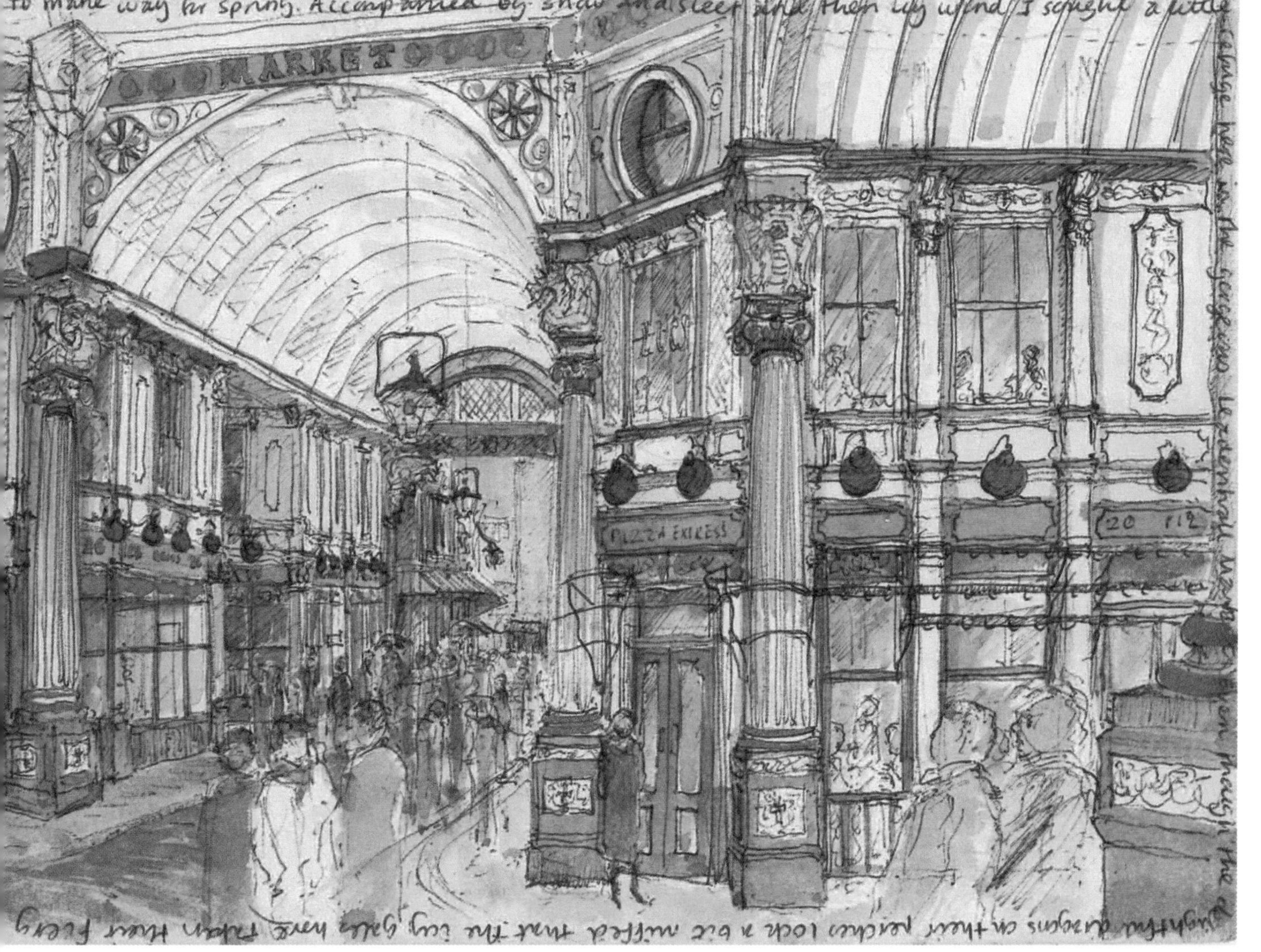
to make way for spring. Accompanied by snow and sleet
I sought a little
refuge here in the sumptuous Leadenhall Market though the
frightful dragons on their perches look a bit miffed that the city gods have taken their fiery
MARKET
PIZZA EXPRESS

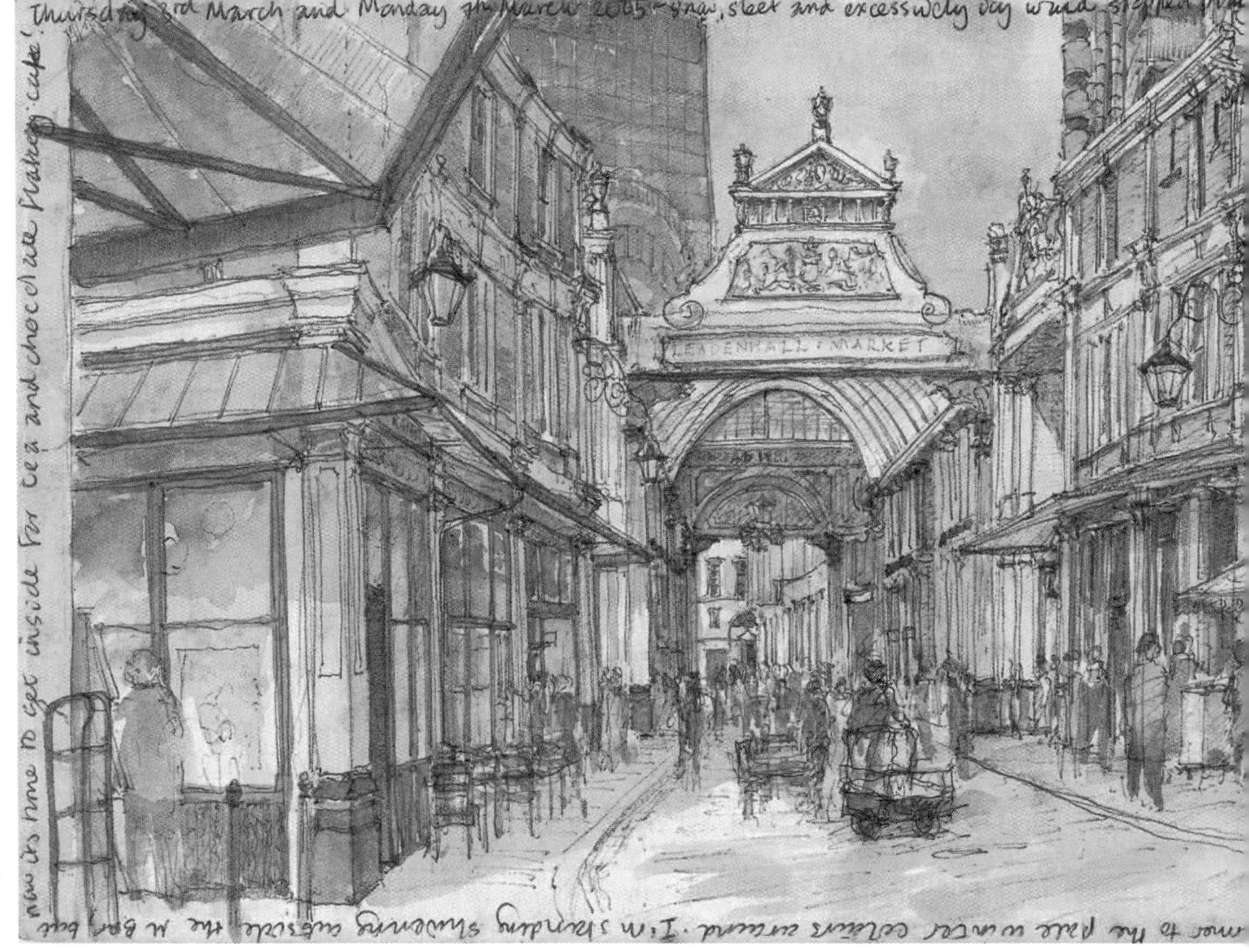
Thursday 3rd March and Monday 7th March 2005 - snow, sleet and excessively dry wind stopped
now it's time to get inside for tea and chocolate Flakes cafe!
LEADENHALL MARKET
to the pale winter colours around. I'm standing shivering outside the M Bar but

3

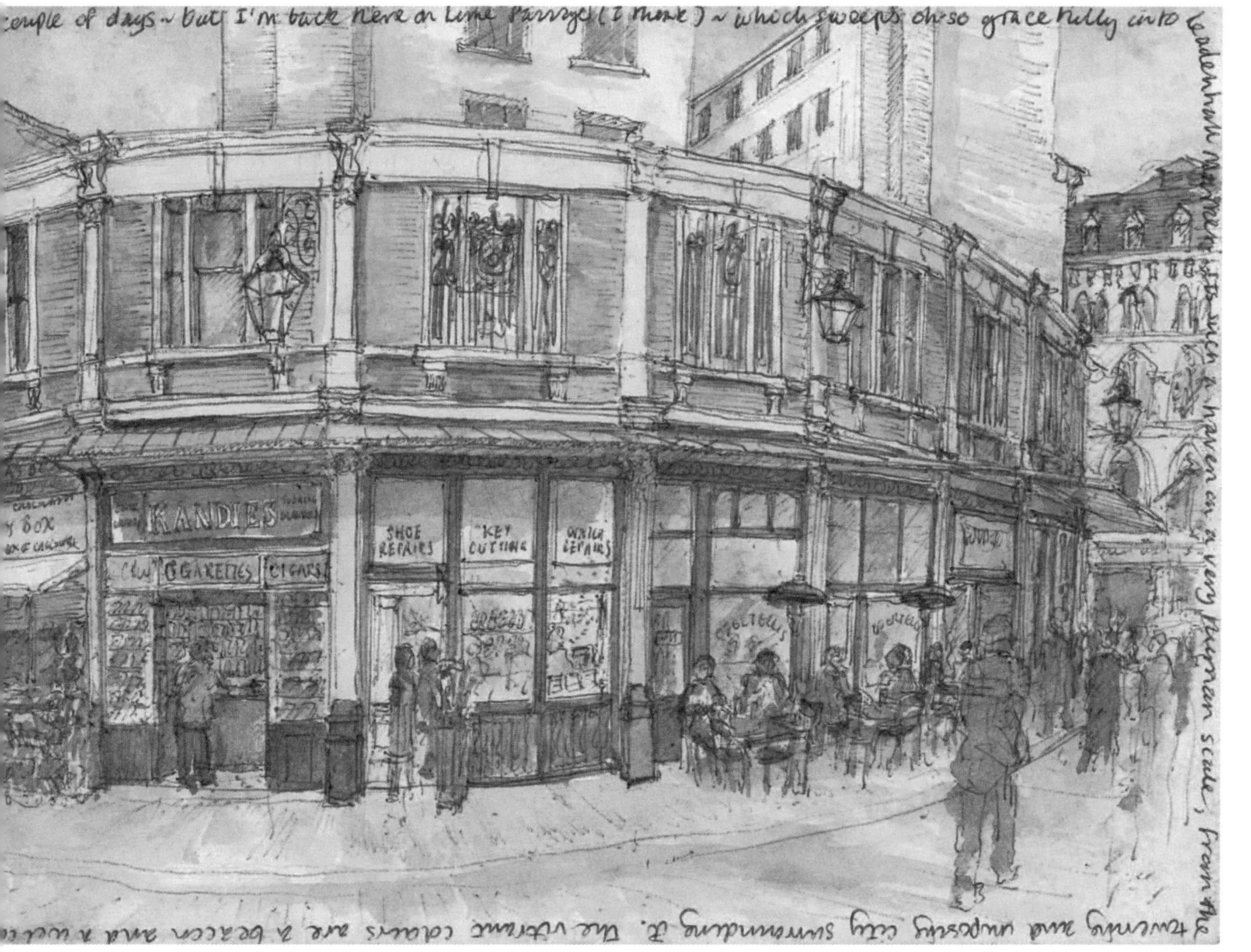
couple of days ~ but I'm back here on Lime Passage (I think) ~ which sweeps oh so gracefully into
Leadenhall Market its such a haven on a very human scale, from the
towering and imposing city surrounding it. The vibrant colours are a beacon and a wel
KANDIES
CIGARETTES
CIGARS
SHOE REPAIRS
KEY CUTTING
WATCH REPAIRS

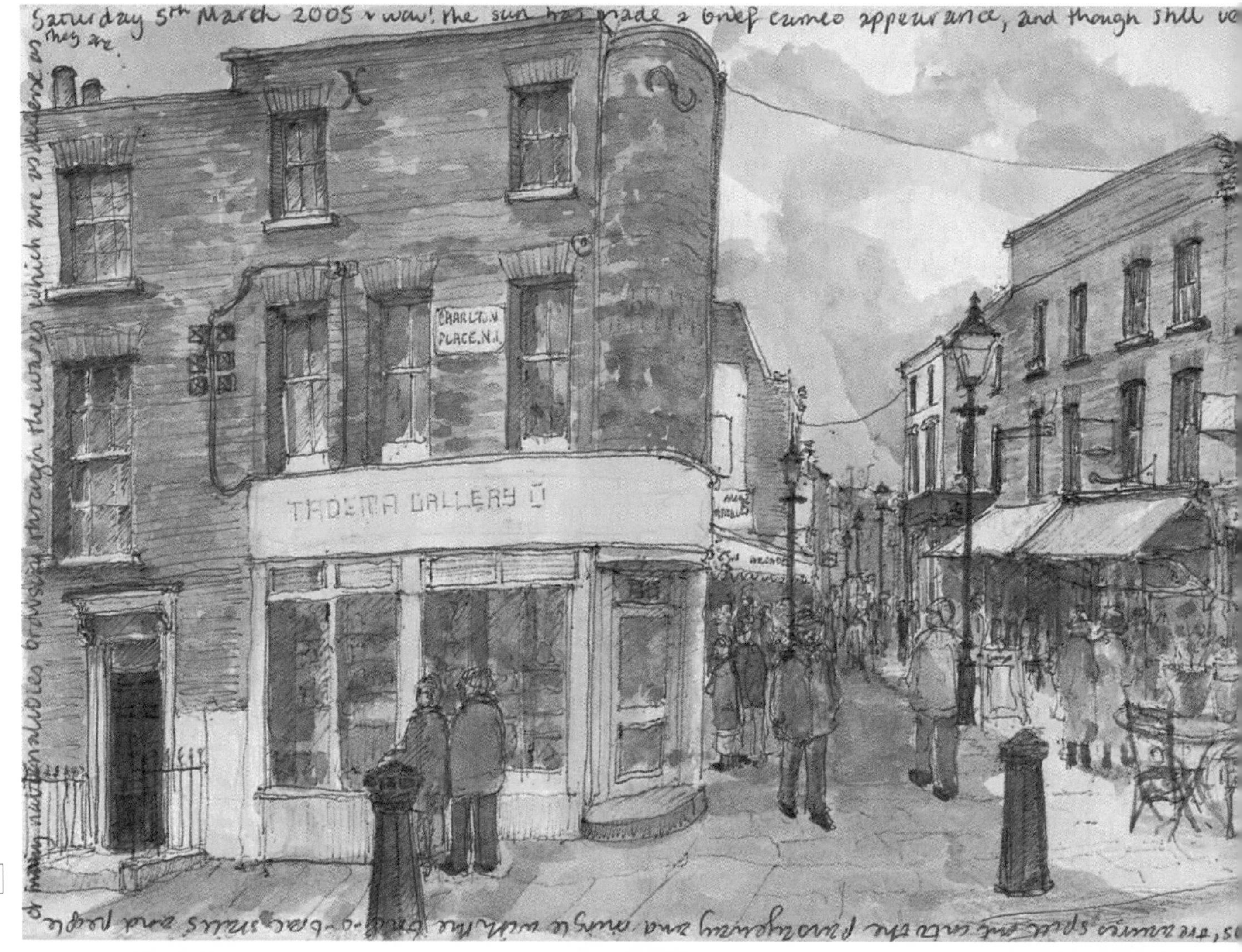
Saturday 5th March 2005 – wow! the sun has made a brief cameo appearance, and though still ve
they are.
CHARLTON PLACE. N.1
TADEMA GALLERY

4

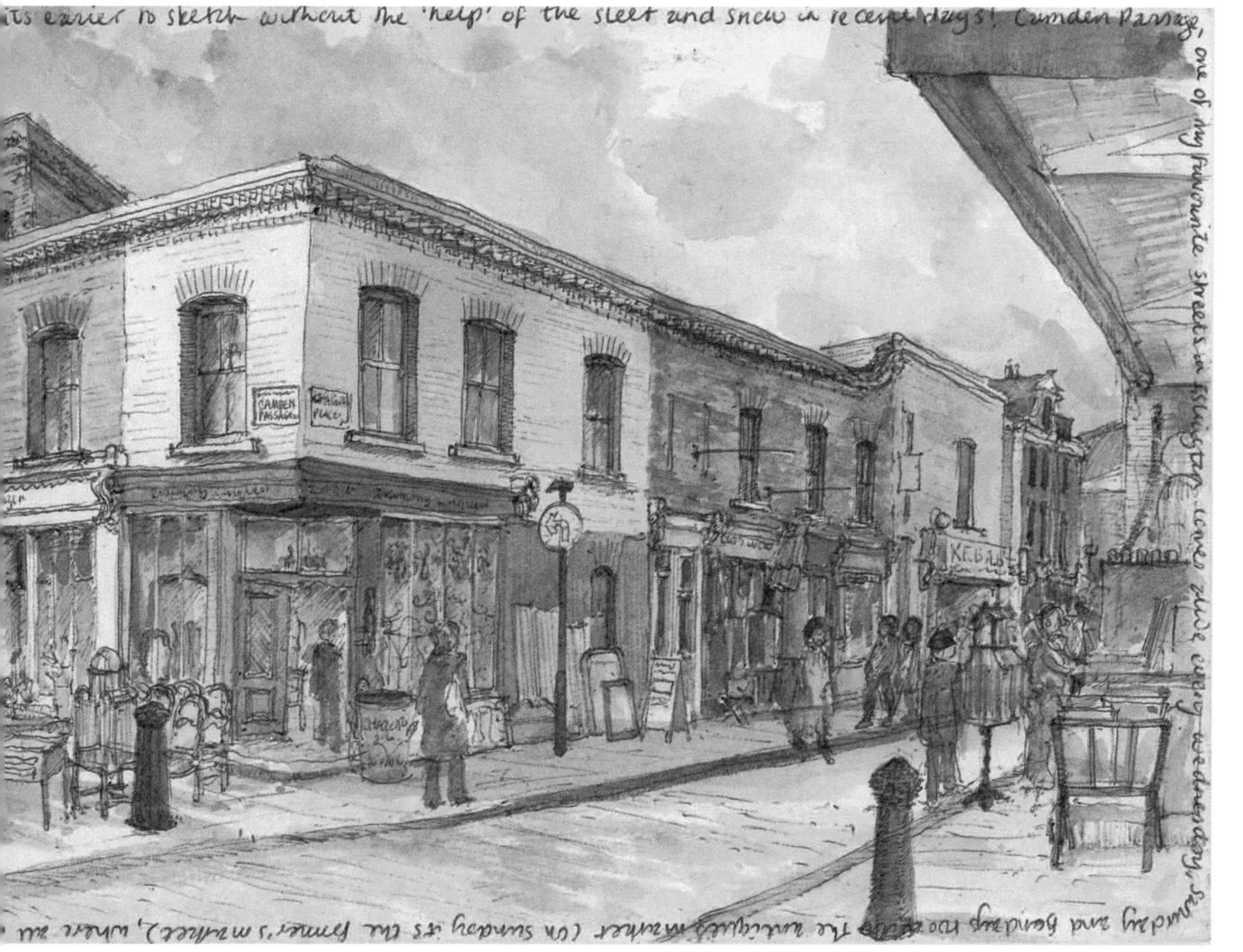
its easier to sketch without the 'help' of the sleet and snow in recent days! Camden Passage,
one of my favourite streets in Islington comes alive every Wednesday, Sa
turday and Sundays the antiques market (on Sunday it's the farmer's market), where all
CAMDEN PASSAGE
KEBABS

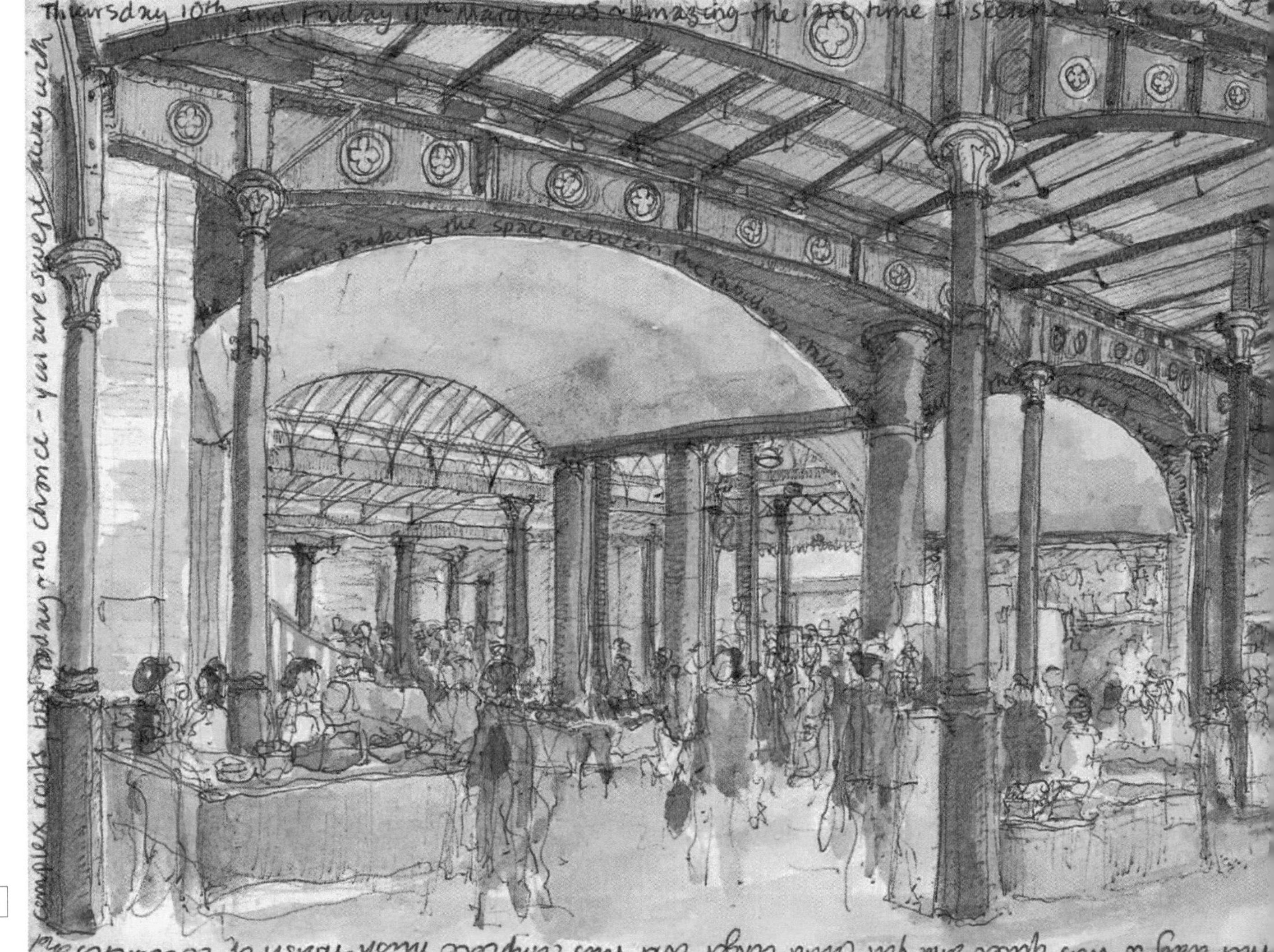

5

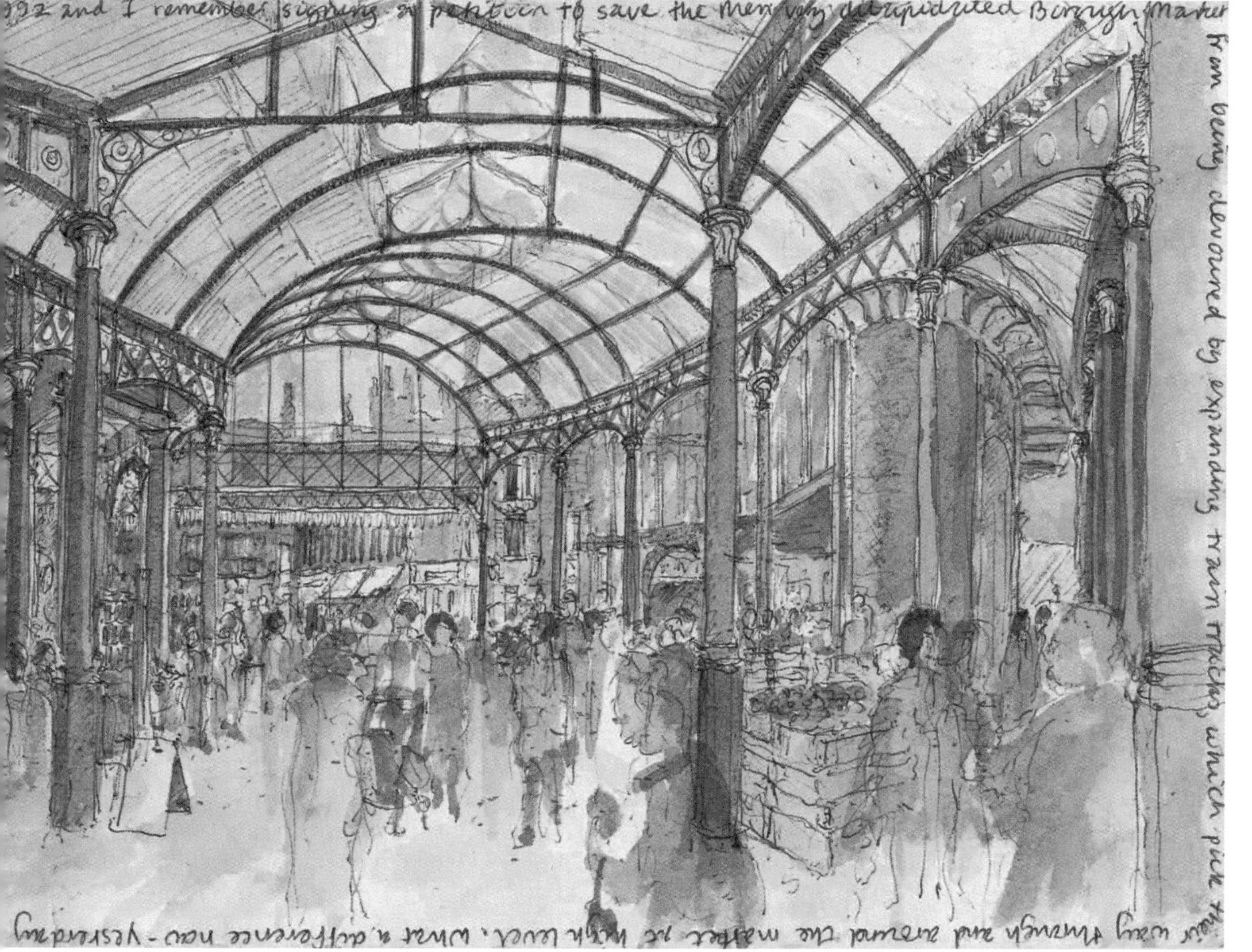
992 and I remember signing a petition to save the then very dilapidated Borough Market
from being devoured by expanding train tracks, which pick
their way through and around the market at high level. What a difference now - yesterday

6

Wednesday 9th March 2005 ~ still grey skies, but no snow or sleet like last week. Also I have

in my sofa - it's just the tops from St. Martin's within Ludgate all the way to

the Nat West Tower and beyond to Sir Norman's new creation..

anyway St. Paul's is still biggest from this angle

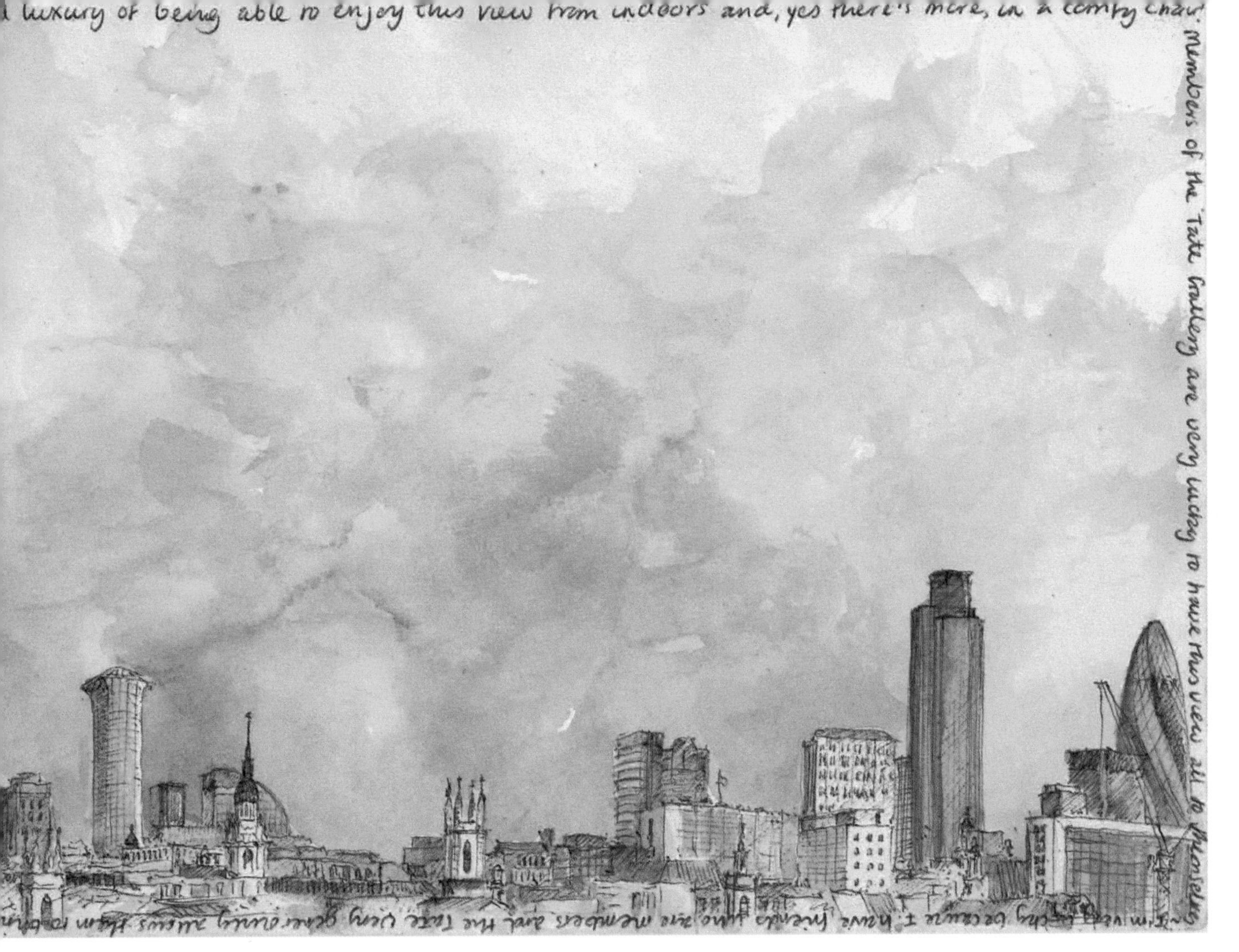
luxury of being able to enjoy this view from indoors and, yes there's more, in a comfy chair!
Members of the Tate Gallery are very lucky to have this view all to themselves
I'm very lucky because I have friends who are members and the Tate very generously allows them to

7

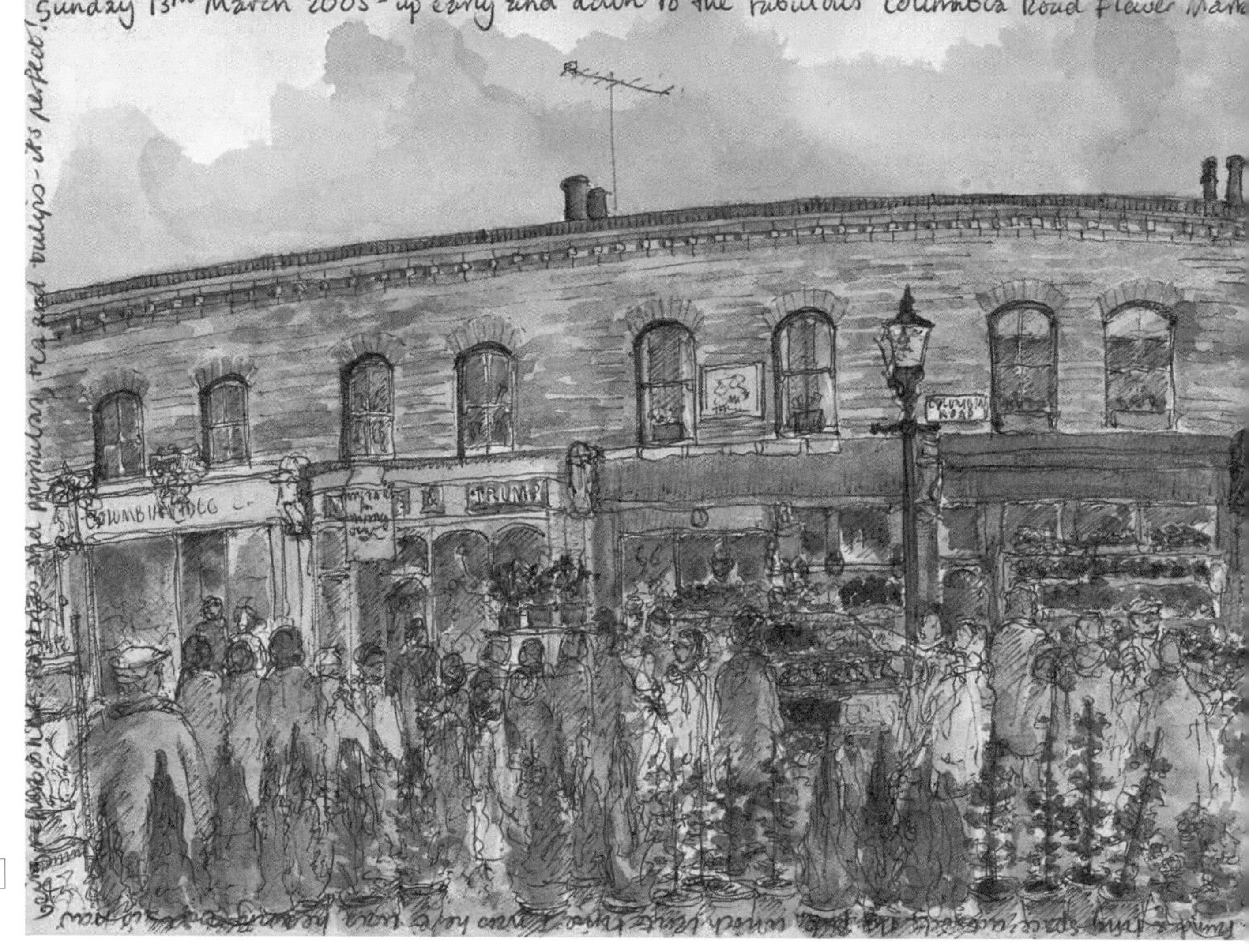

Sunday 13th March 2005 - up early and down to the fabulous Columbia Road Flower Mark
TRUMP
COLUMBIA ROAD

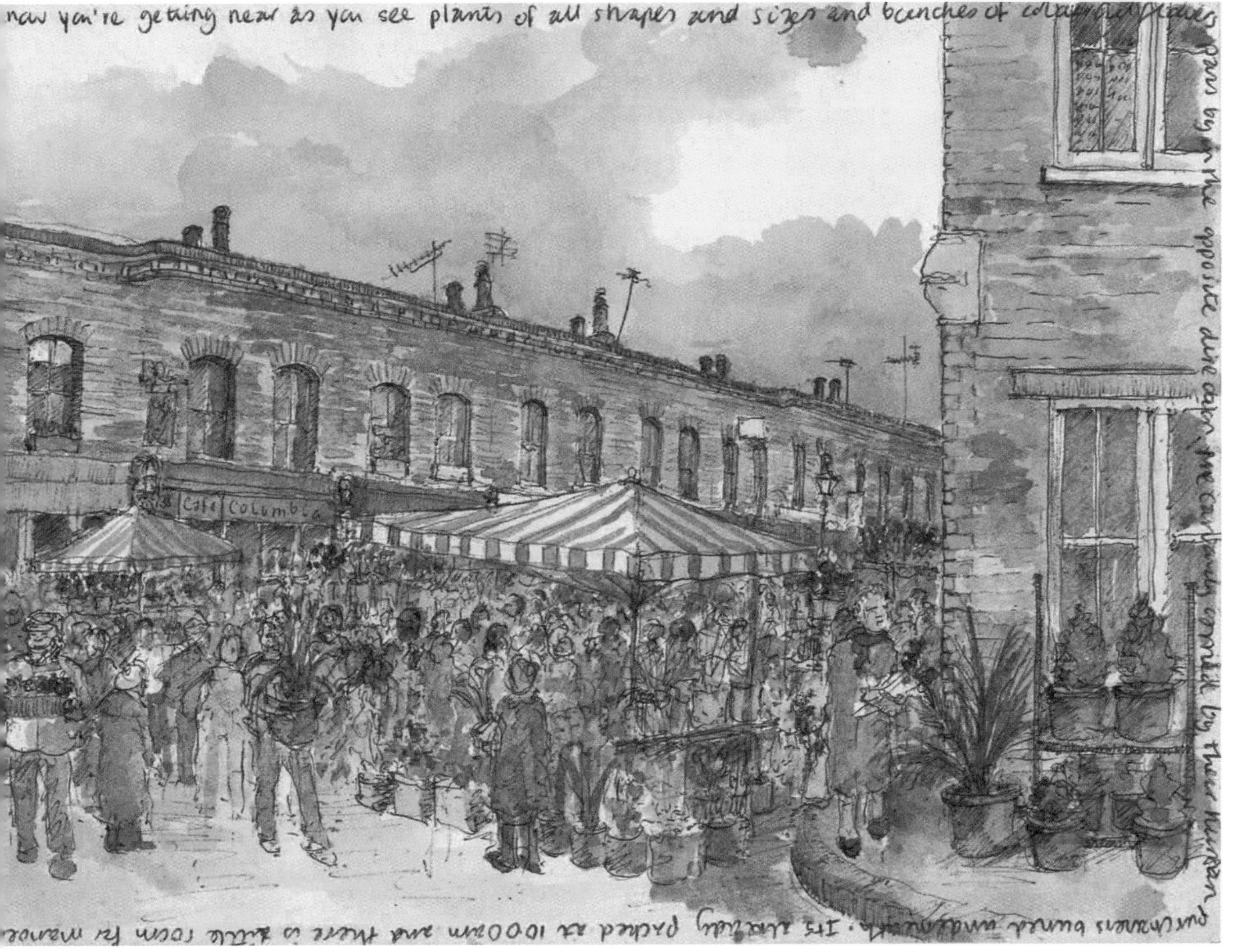
now you're getting near as you see plants of all shapes and sizes and bunches of
pass by in the opposite direction
purchasers buried underneath. It's amazingly packed at 10.00am and there is little room for manoe
Cafe Columbia

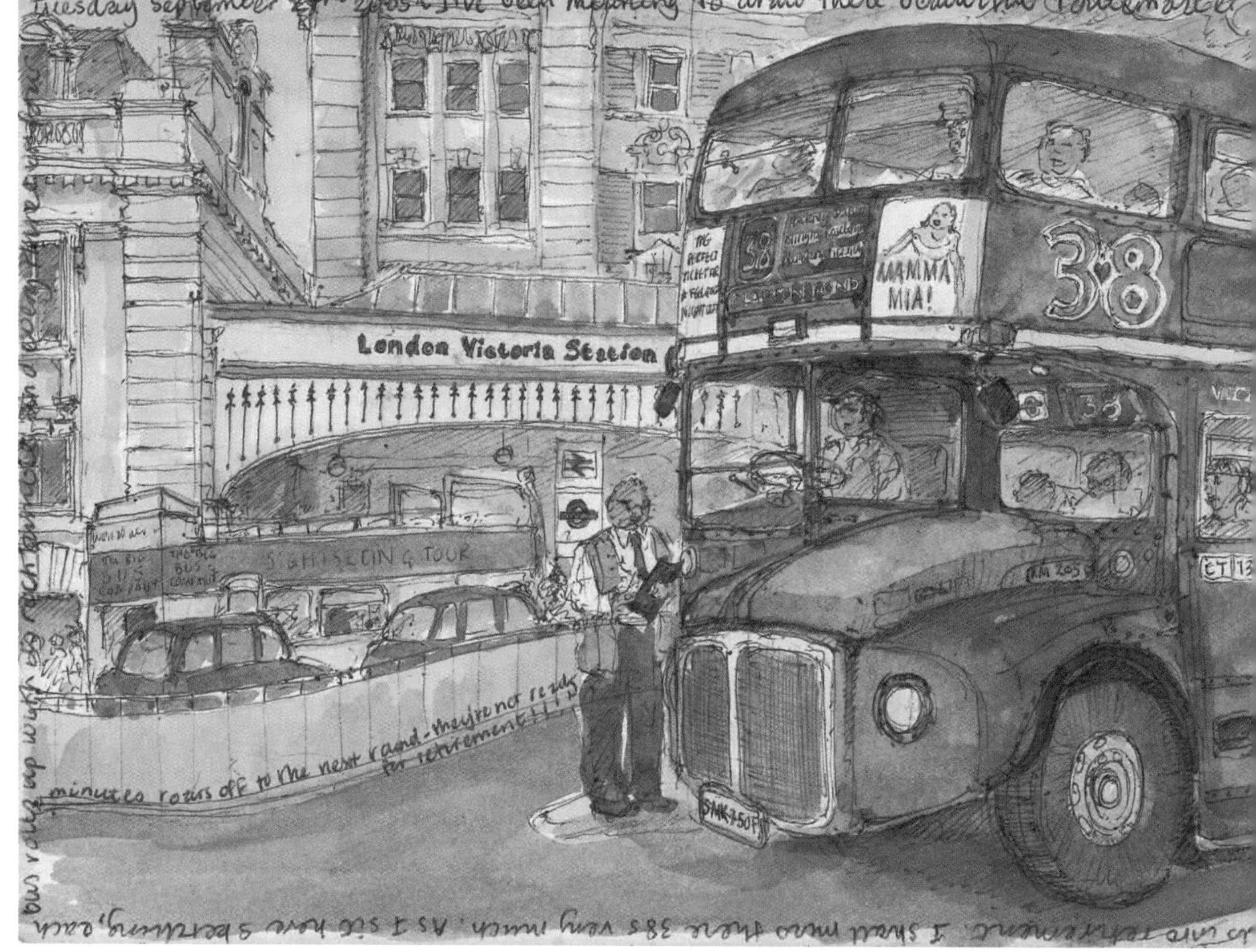
Tuesday September 27th 2005 - I've been meaning to draw these beautiful Routemaster
London Victoria Station
38
MAMMA MIA!
SIGHTSEEING TOUR
minutes roars off to the next round - they're not ready for retirement!!!

8

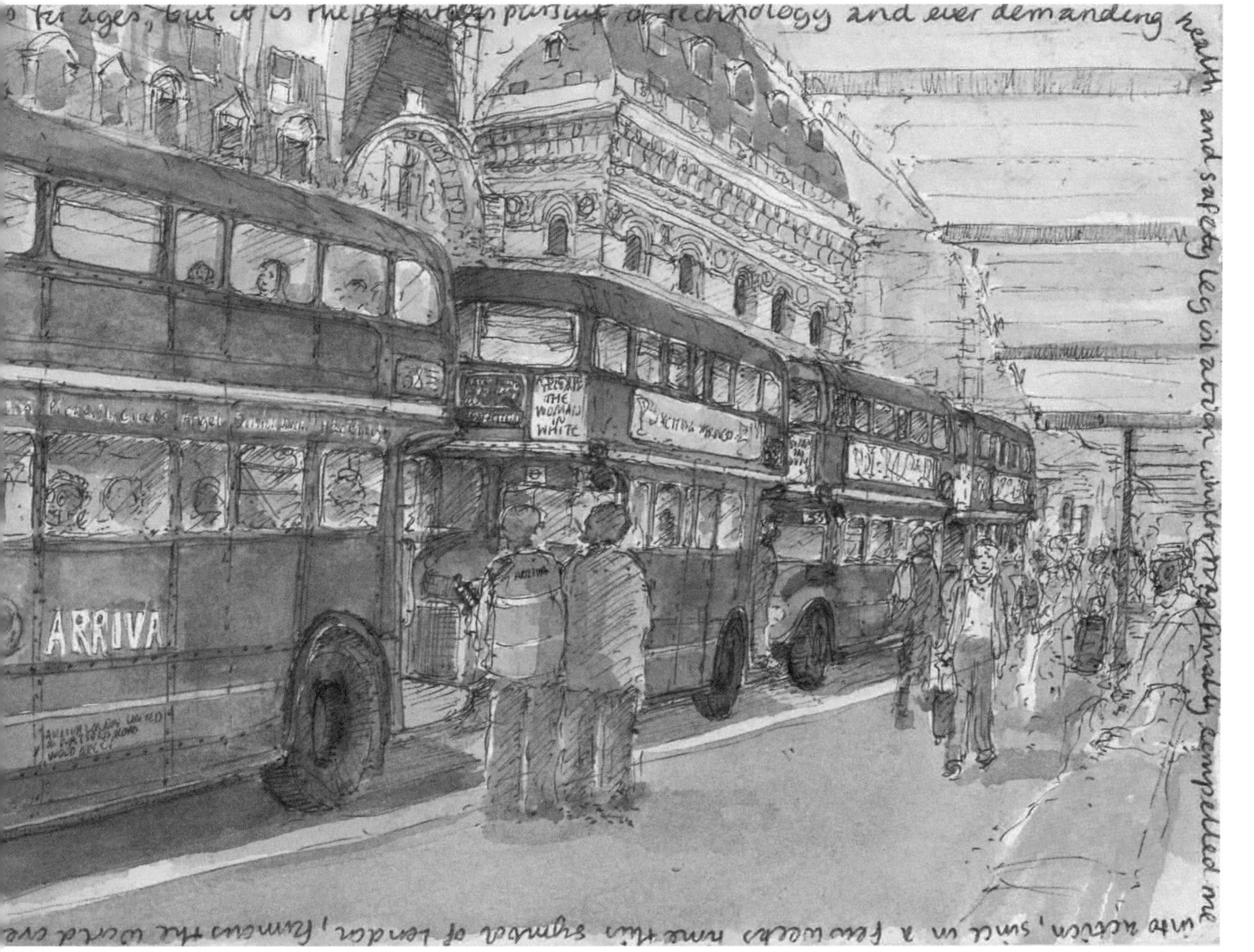
o for ages, but it is the
pursuit of technology and ever demanding health
and safety legislation which has finally compelled me
into action, since in a few weeks time this symbol of London, famous the world ove
THE WOMAN IN WHITE
ARRIVA
ARRIVA

Monday October 2nd 2005 ~ just a few minutes from the end of the no. 38 bus route at Clapton

be revived and restored so they can run and roar off into the relentless travelling

9 traffic. By the end of the month this sight will be gone, and they'll

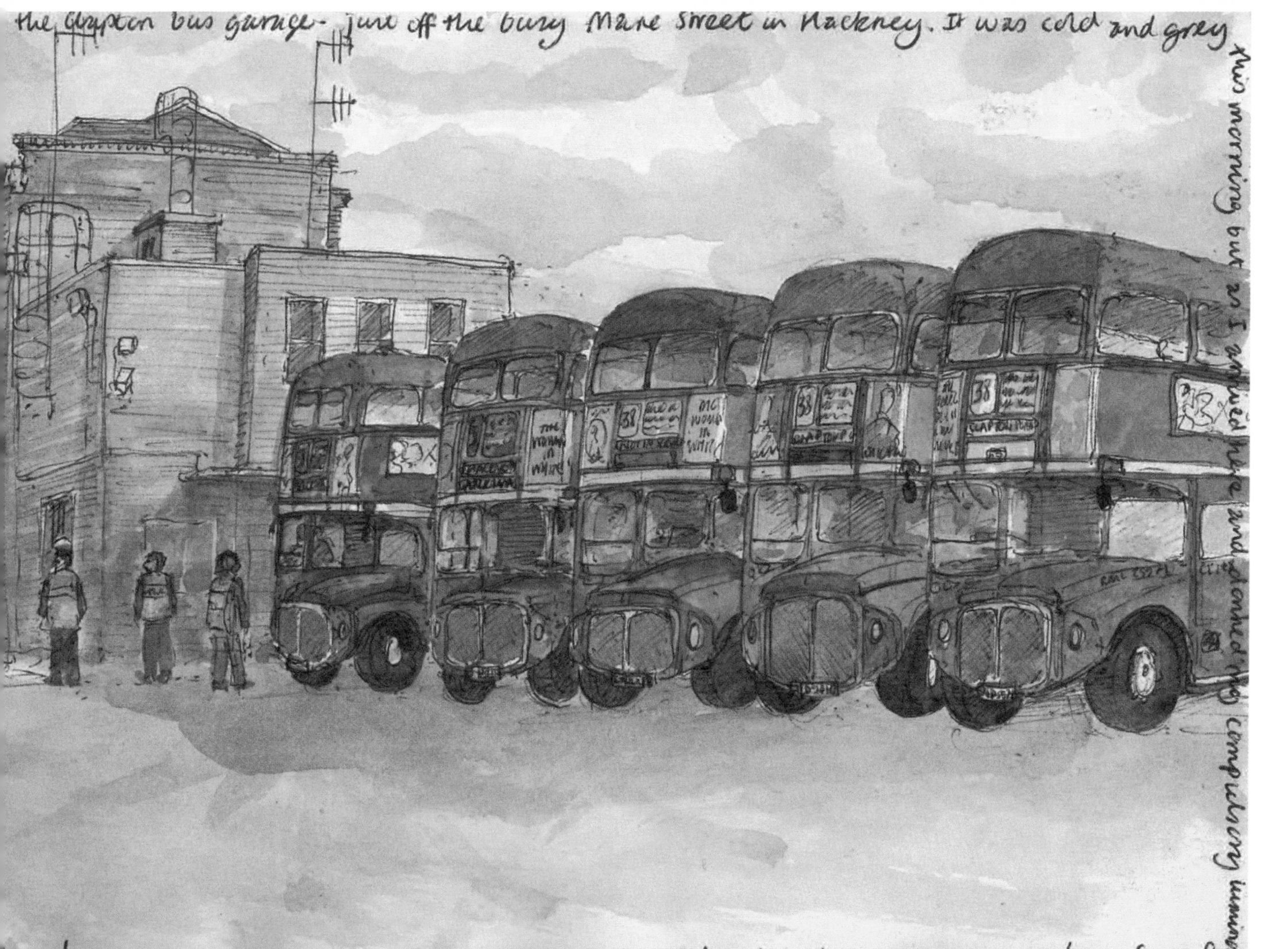
the Clapton bus garage - just off the busy Mare Street in Hackney. It was cold and grey
this morning but as I arrived here and donned the compulsory luminous
green jacket, the sun came out for a fine few hours. this is where the buses come to rest,

10

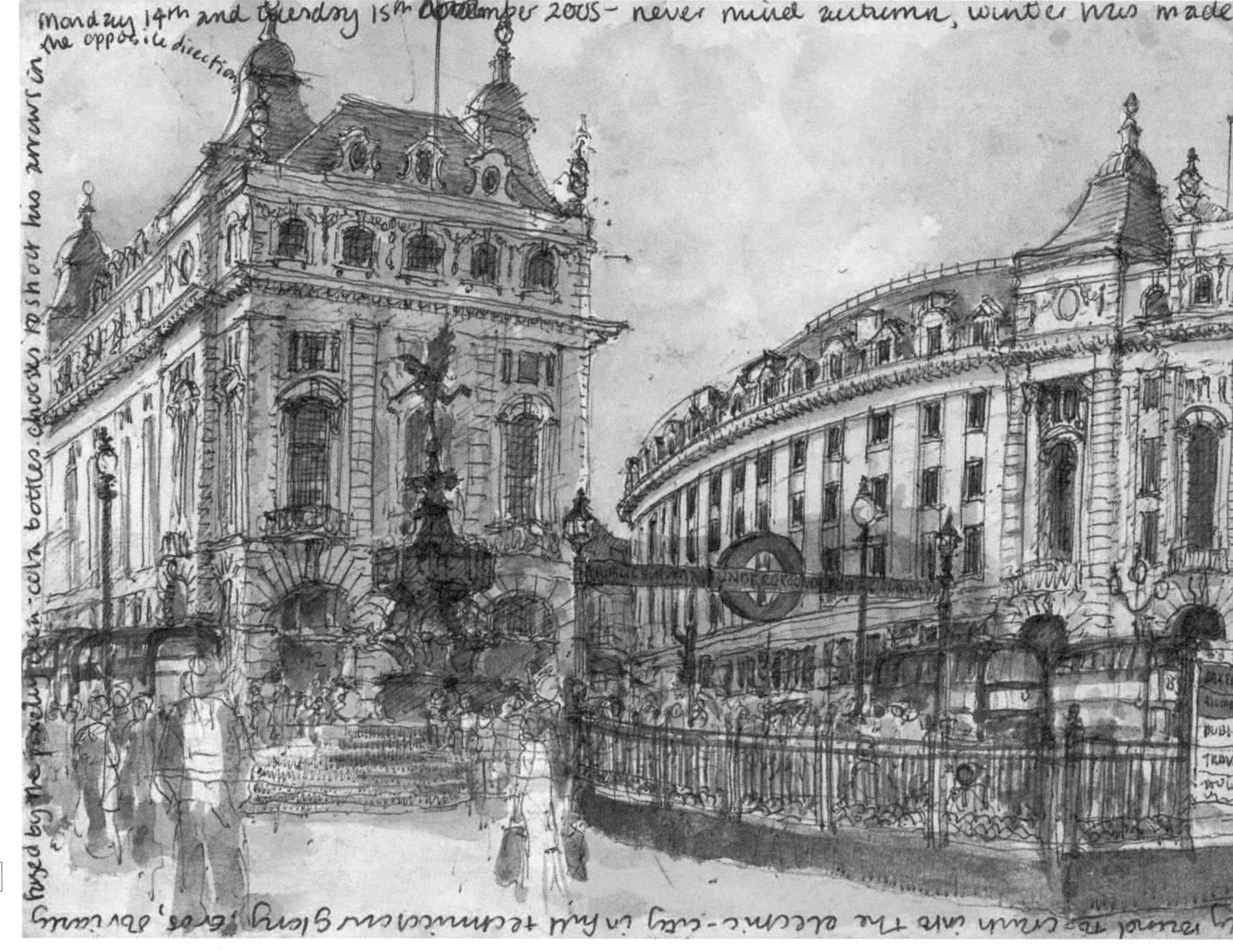
Monday 14th and Tuesday 15th November 2005 - never mind autumn, winter has made
the opposite direction
coca-cola bottles. chooses to shoot his arrows in
the electric city in full technicolour glory. Eros, obviously

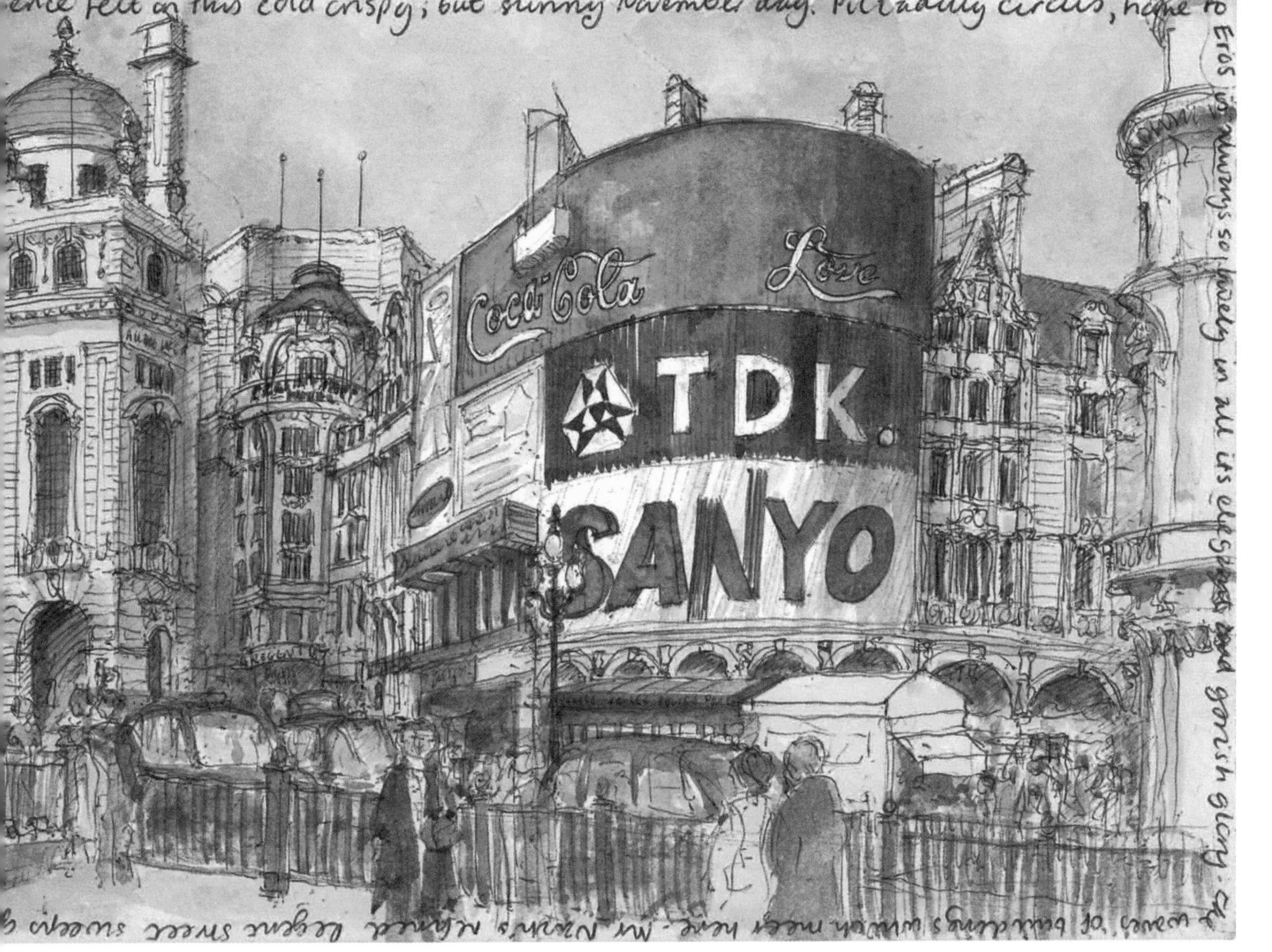
ence felt on this cold crispy; but sunny November day. Piccadilly circus, home to
Coca-Cola
Love
TDK.
SANYO

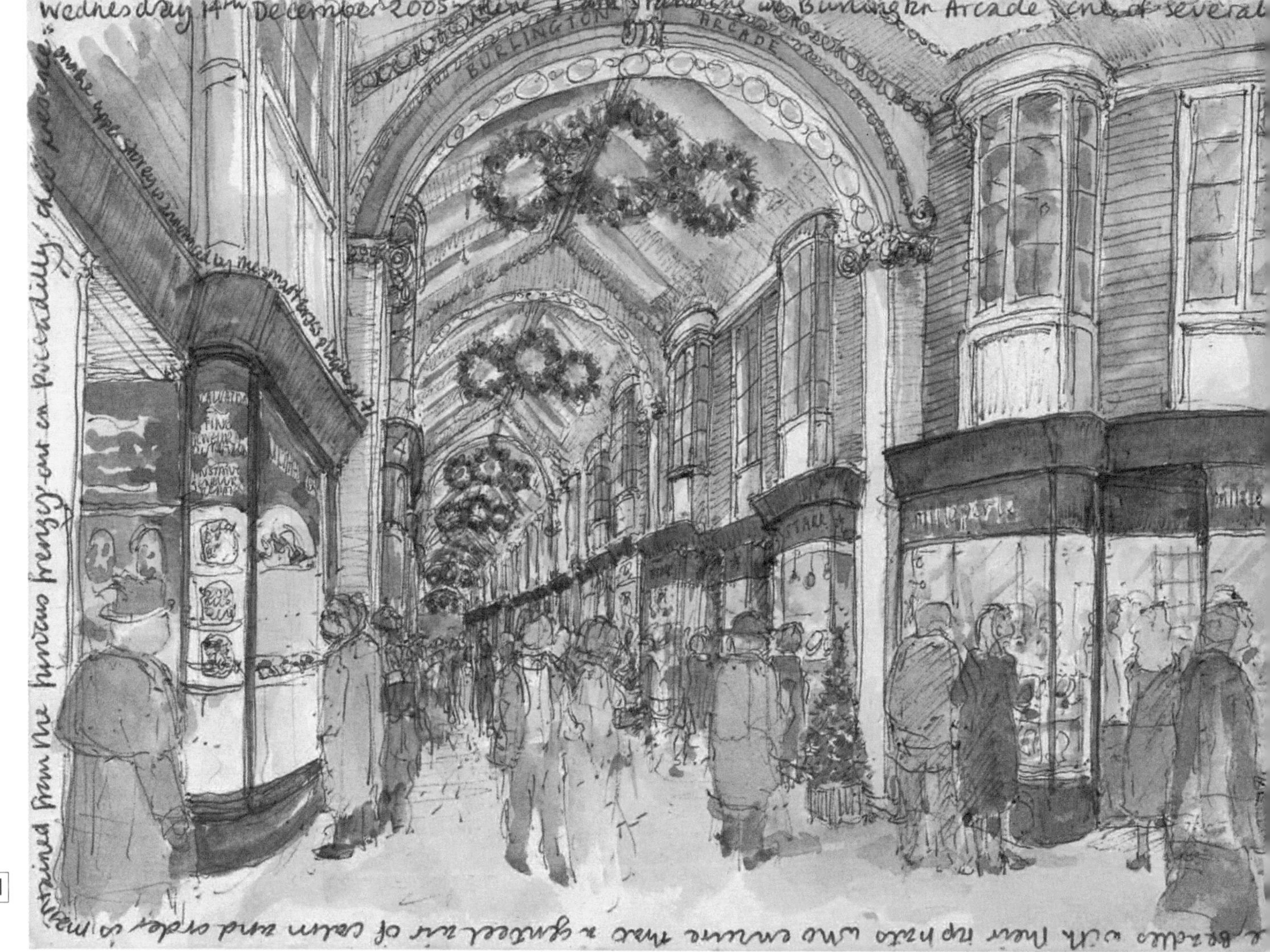
Wednesday 14th December 2005
BURLINGTON
ARCADE
maintained from the hideous frenzy-out on Piccadilly

11

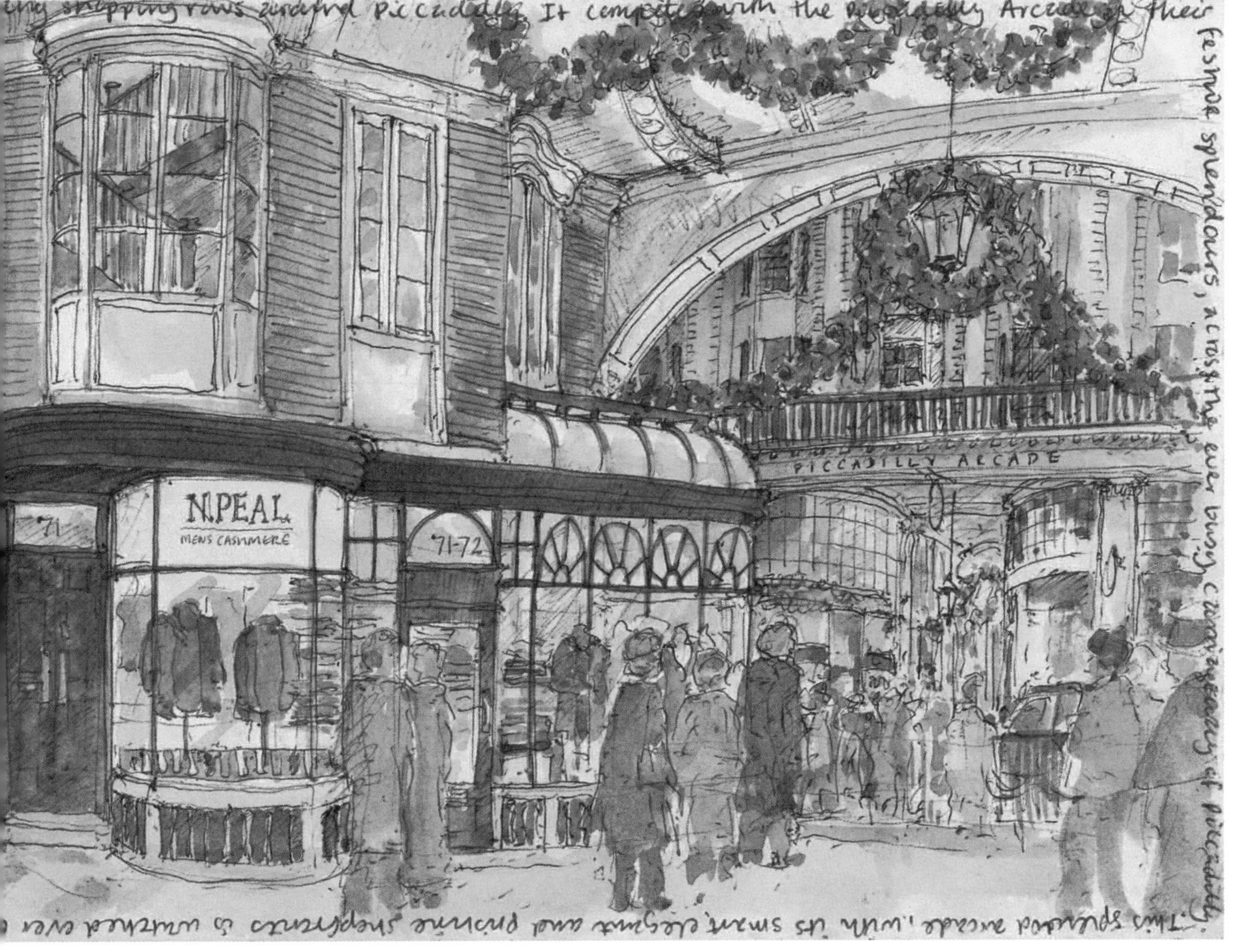
N.PEAL
MENS CASHMERE
71
71-72
PICCADILLY ARCADE

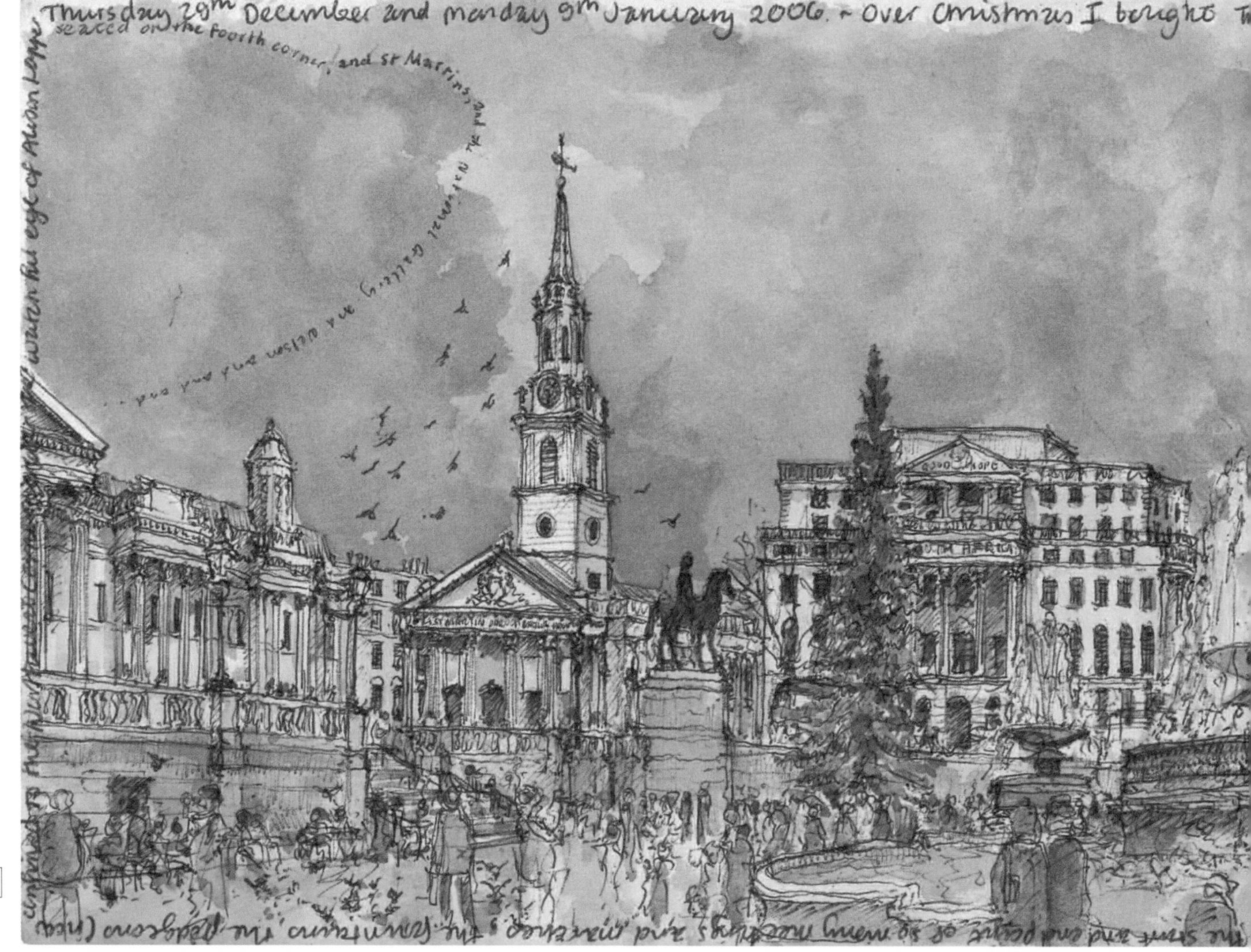
Thursday 29th December and Monday 9th January 2006. – Over Christmas I bought
seated on the fourth corner, and St Martins, and

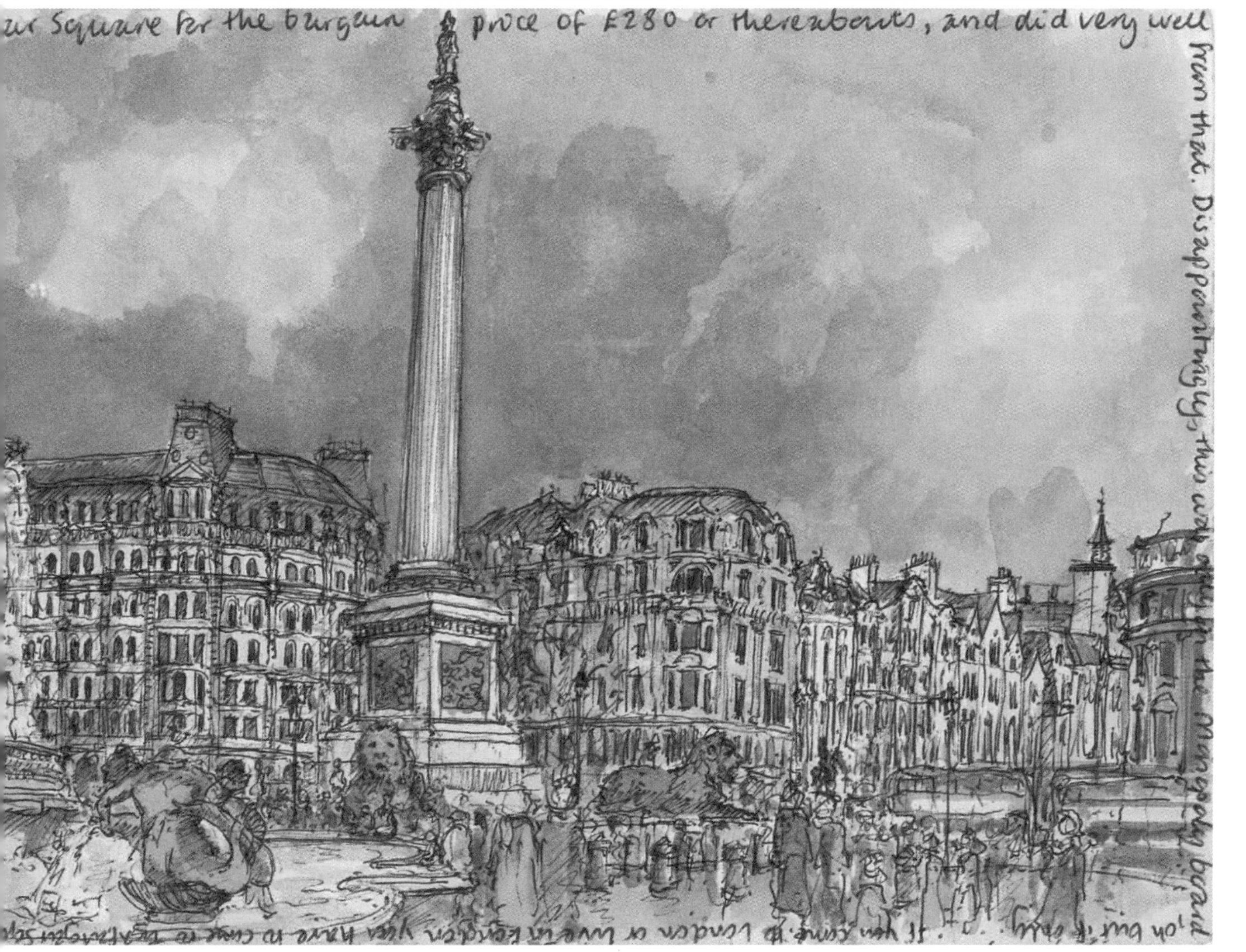
ar Square for the bargain price of £280 or thereabouts, and did very well
from that. Disappointingly, this was only in the Monopoly board
, oh but if only . . . If you come to London or live in London you have to come to Trafalgar Sq

13

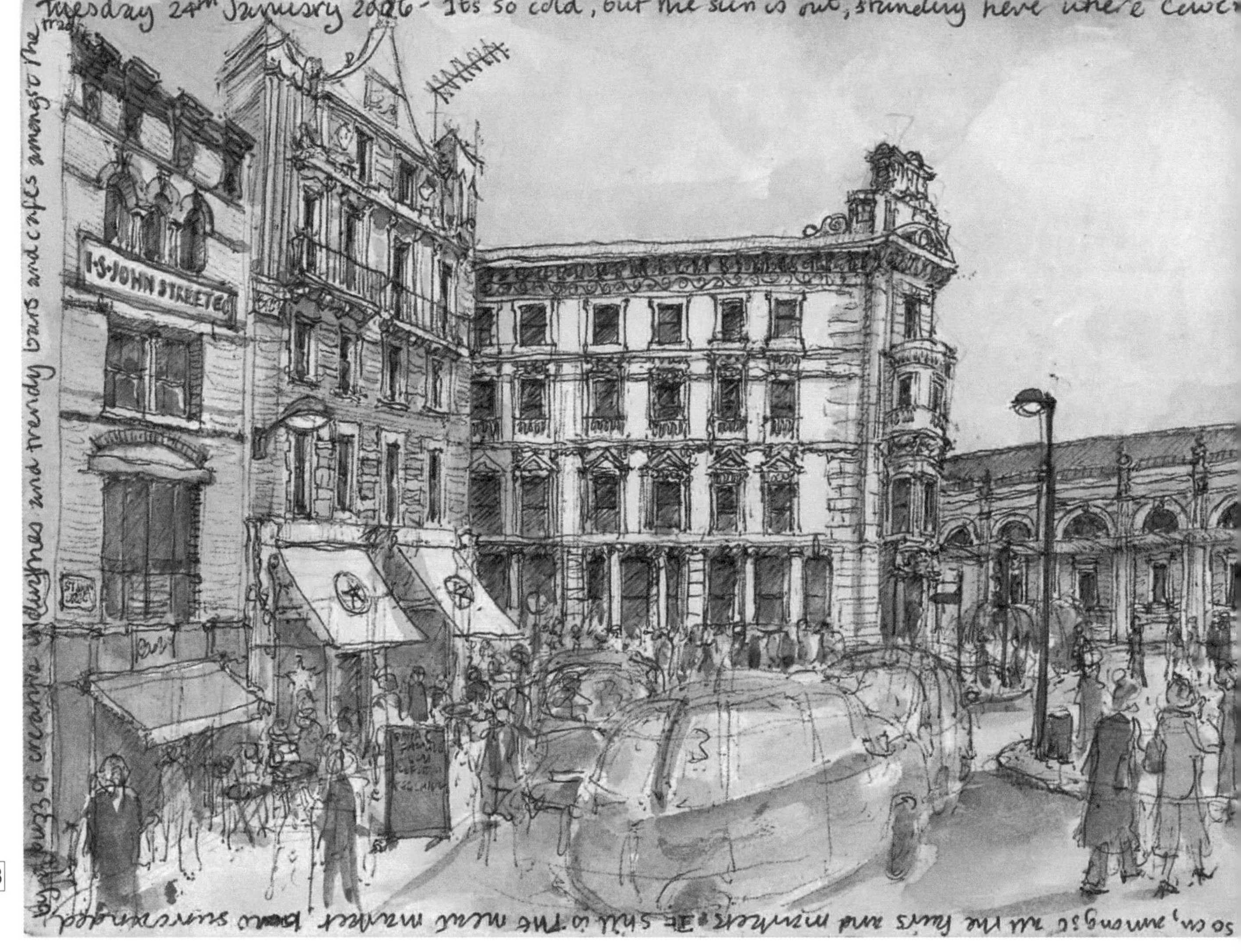
Tuesday 24th January 2006 - Its so cold, but the sun is out, standing here where
1.S.JOHN STREET EC1

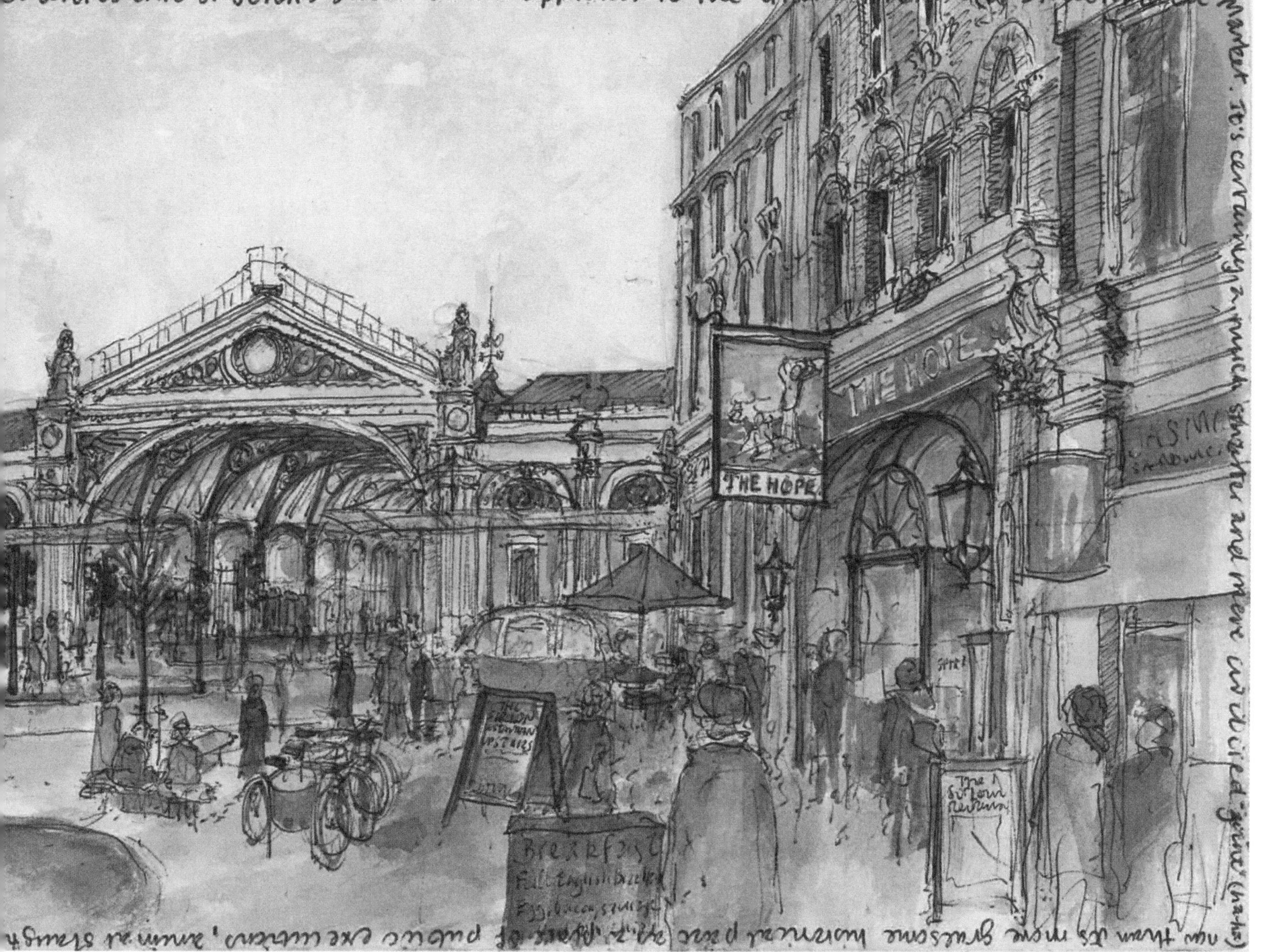

et drifts into St John's Street on the approach to the
market. It's certainly a much smarter and more civilised
now than its more gruesome historical past as the place of public executions, animal slaught
THE HOPE
THE HOPE
Breakfast
Full English breakfast
Egg, bacon, sausage

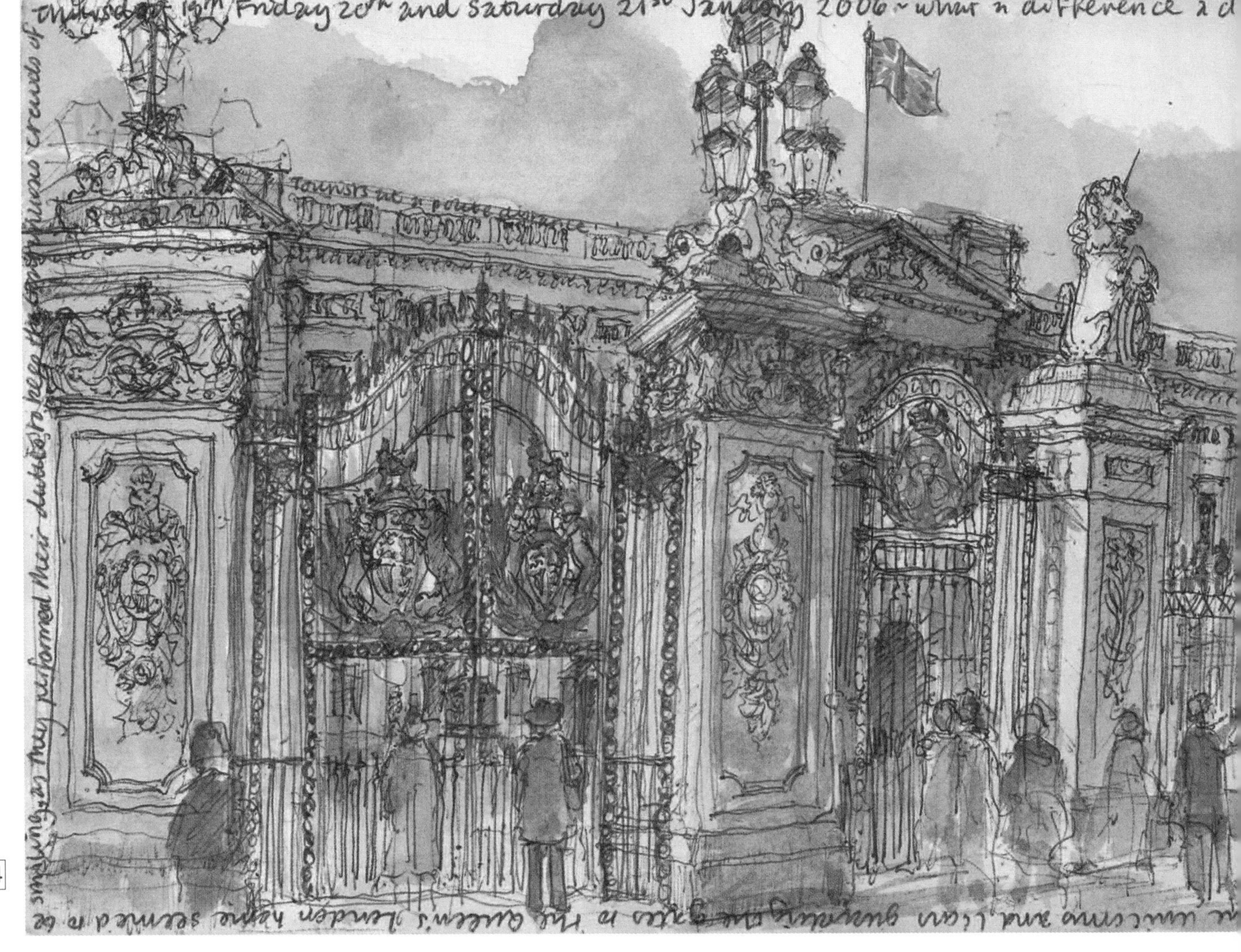
Friday 20th and Saturday 21st January 2006 ~ what a difference

14

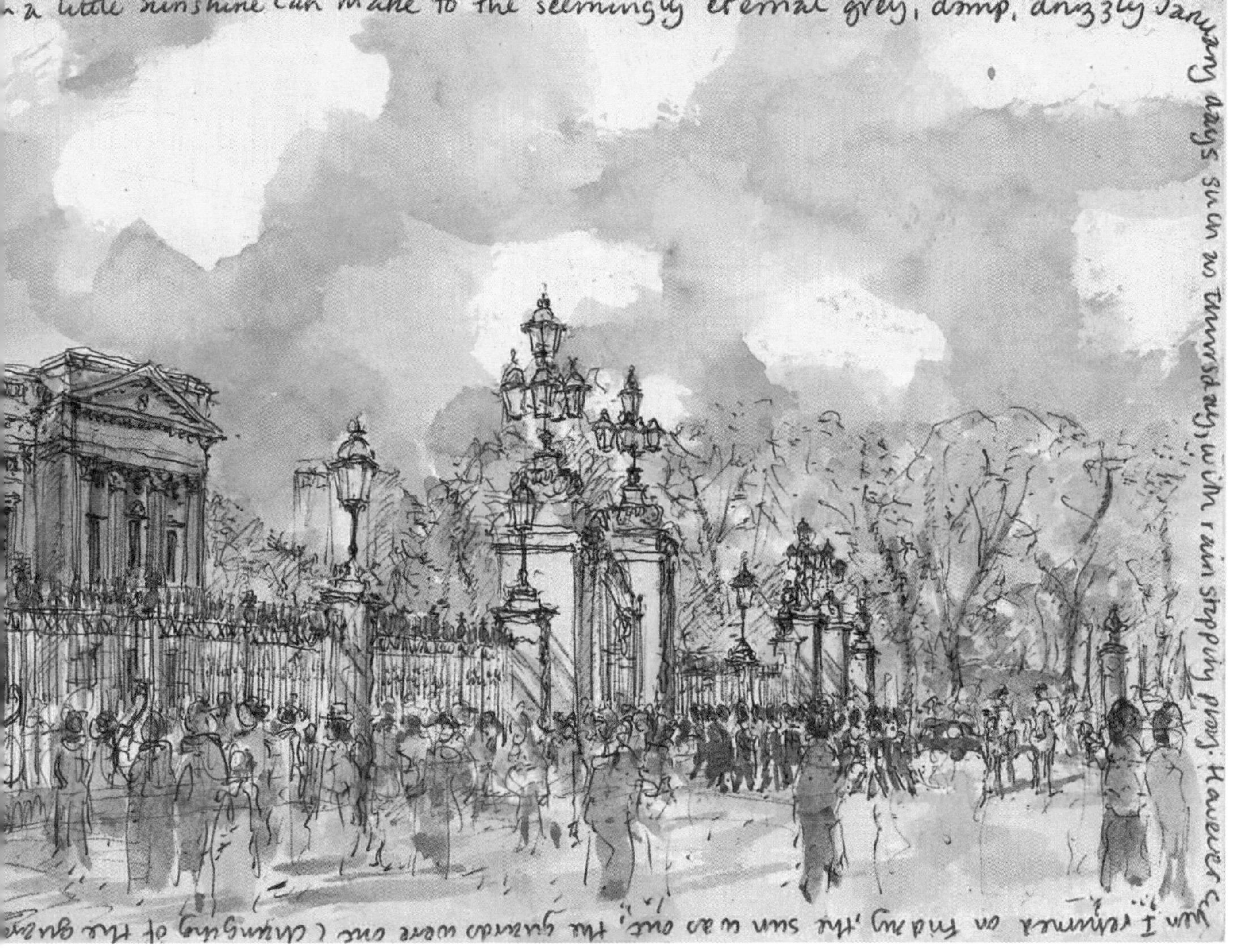
a little sunshine can make to the seemingly eternal grey, damp, drizzly January
days such as Thursday with rain stopping play. However
when I returned on Friday, the sun was out, the guards were out (changing of the guar

15

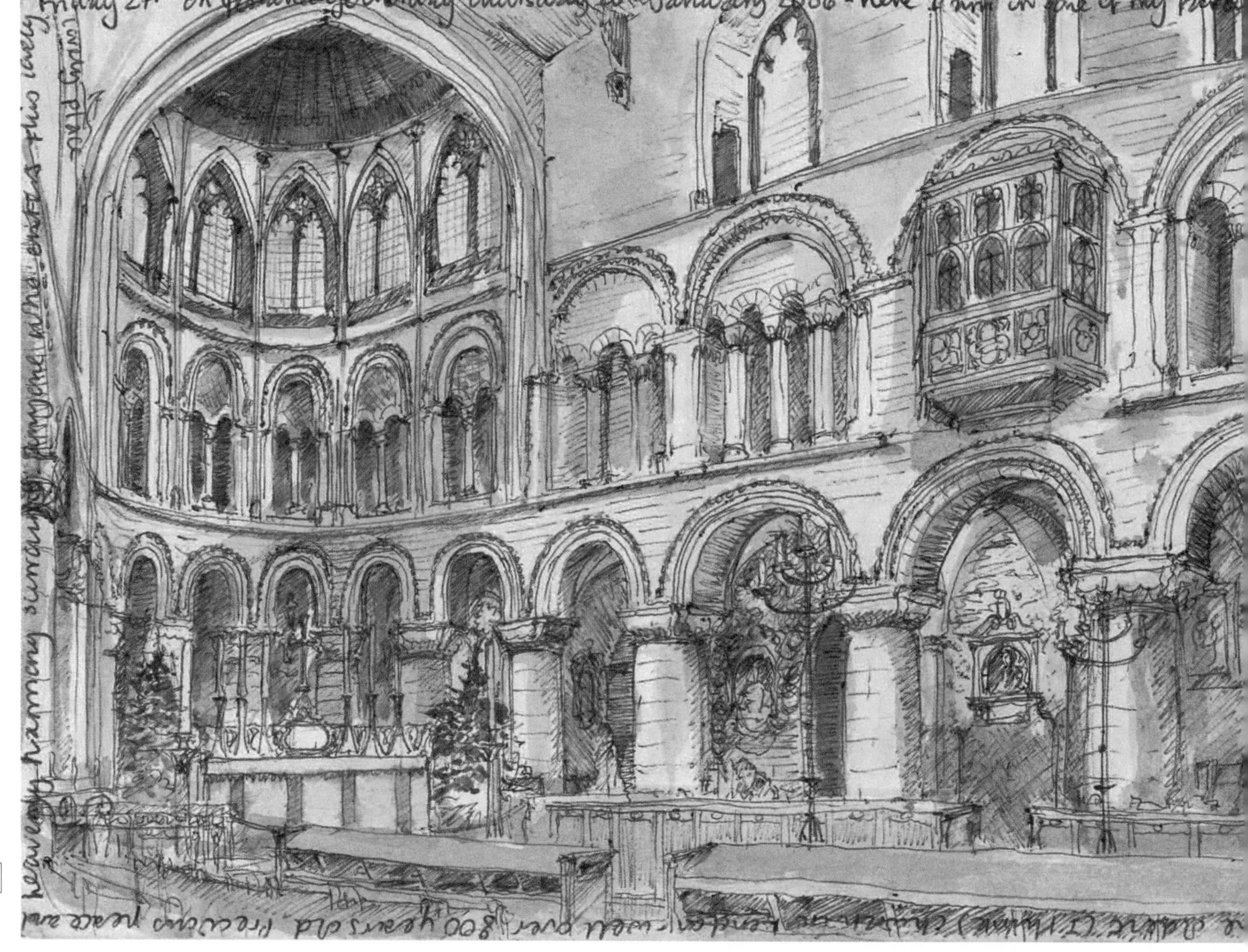

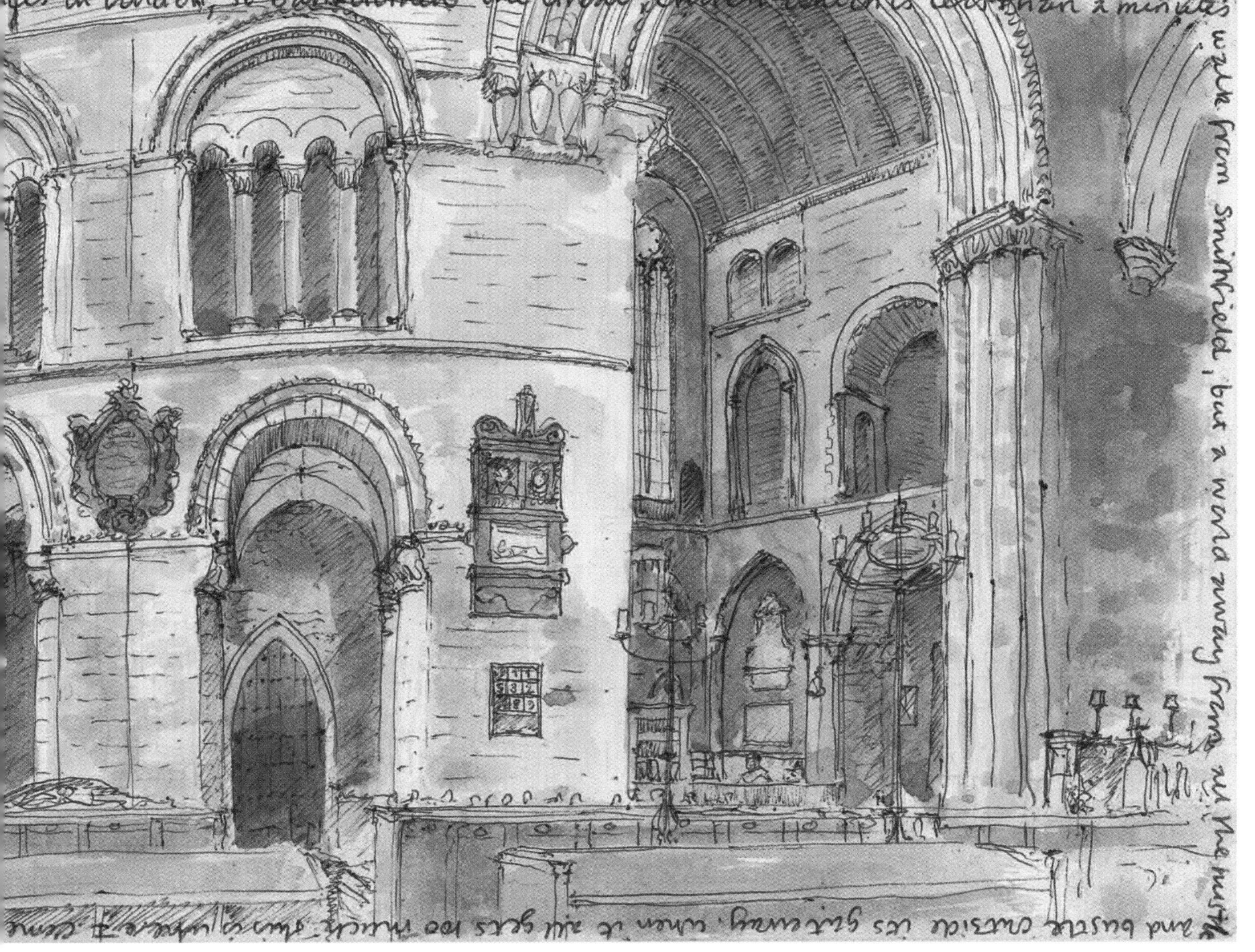
in London, St Bartholomew - the
a minute's
walk from Smithfield, but a world away from all the hustle
and bustle outside

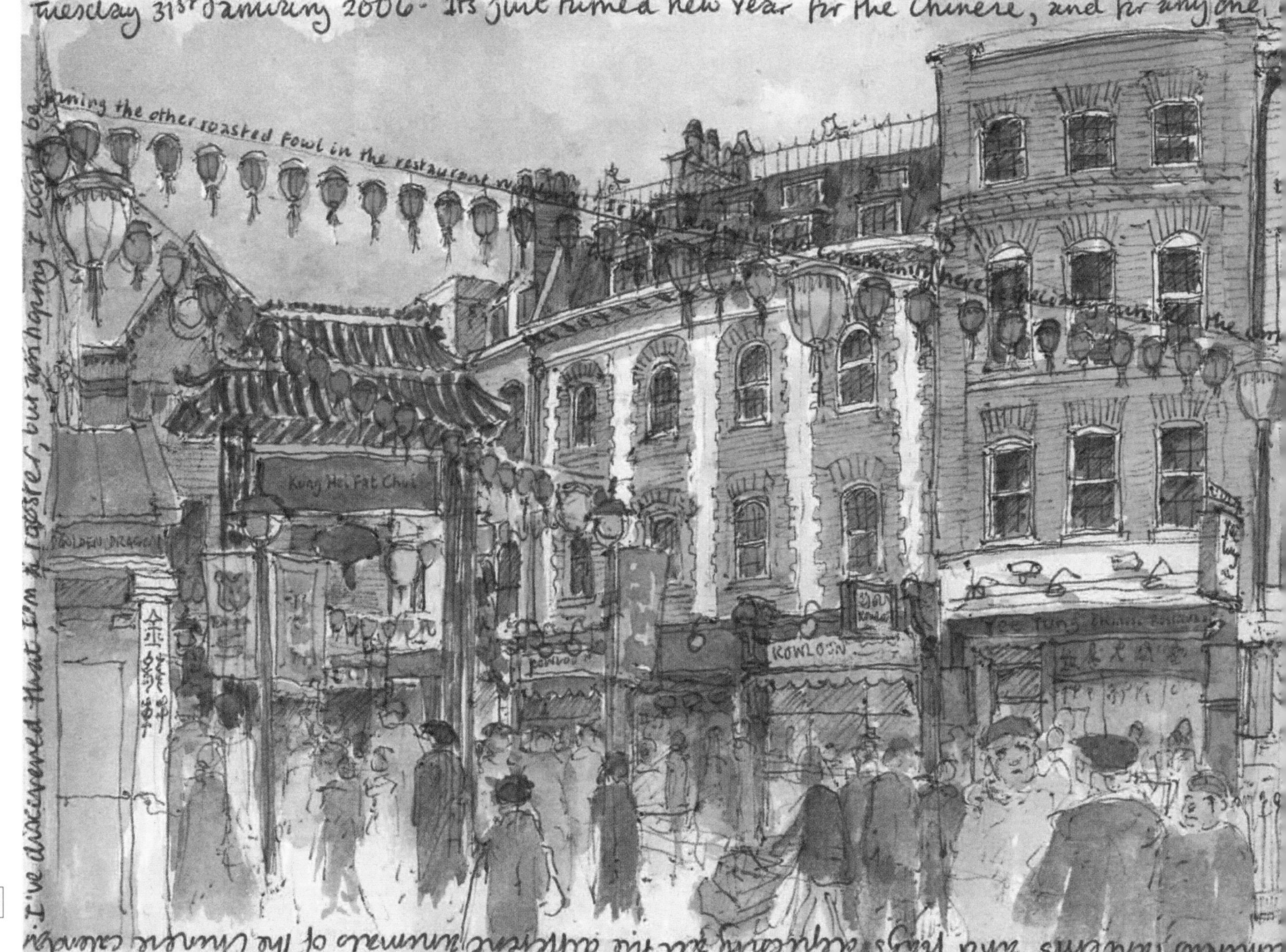
Tuesday 31st January 2006 - It's just turned New Year for the Chinese, and for anyone
I've discovered that I'm a rooster, but was hoping I would be
the other roasted fowl in the restaurant
lanterns and flags depicting all the different animals of the Chinese calendar
Kung Hei Fat Choi
GOLDEN DRAGON
KOWLOON

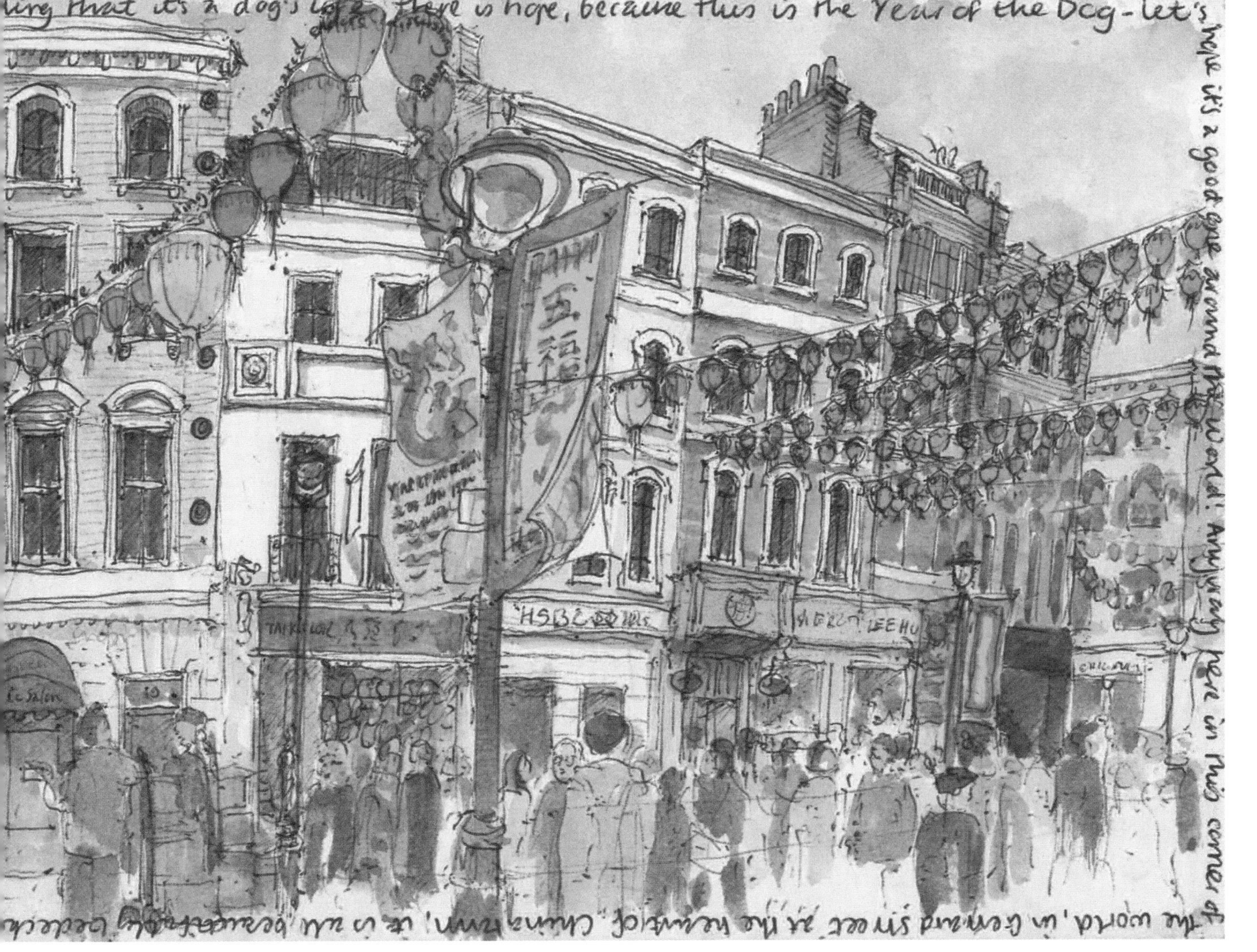
ling that it's a dog's life, there is hope, because this is the Year of the Dog - let's
hope it's a good one around the World! Anyway here in this corner of
the world, in Gerrard Street at the heart of Chinatown, it is all beautifully bedeck
HSBC
LEE HU

17

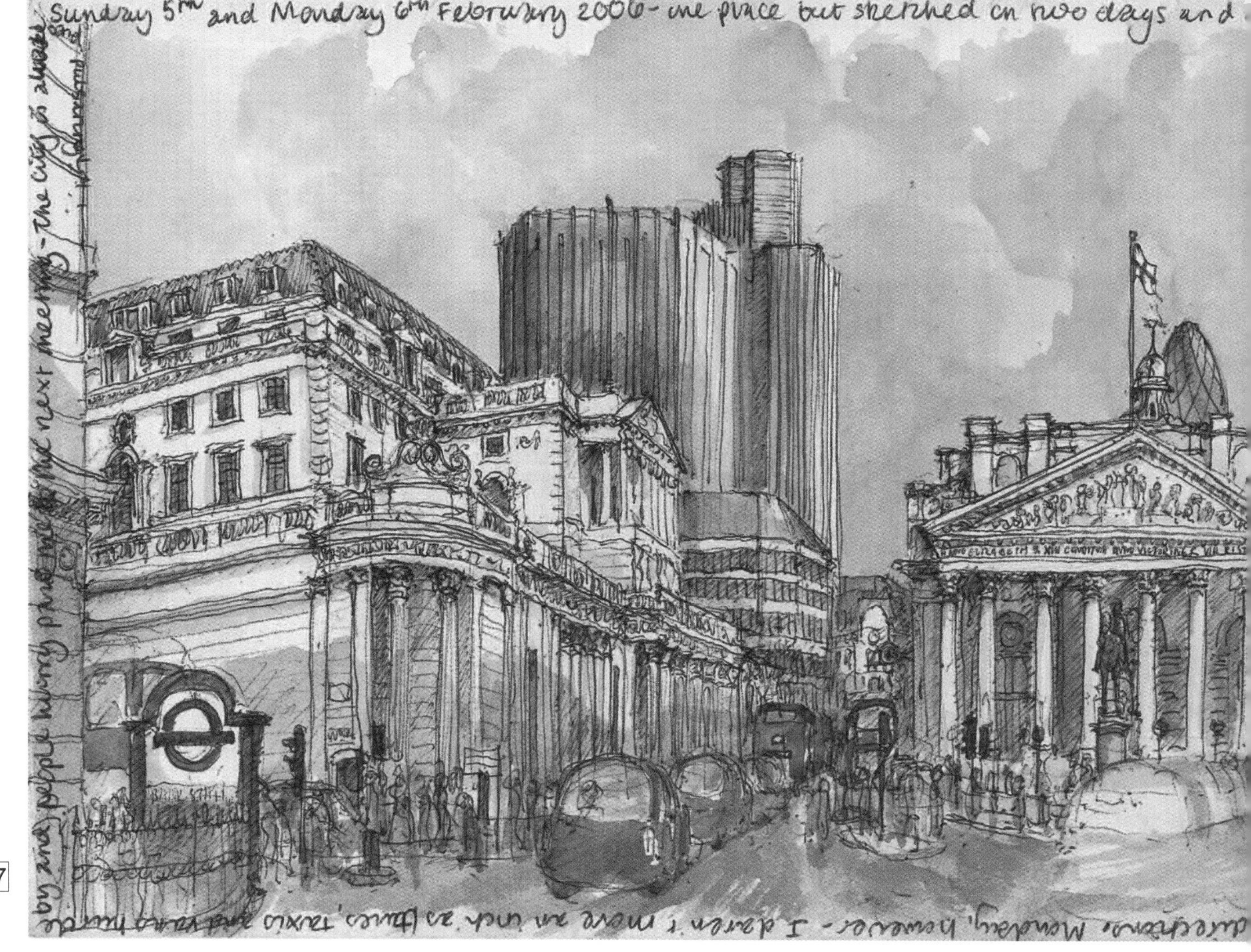
Sunday 5th and Monday 6th February 2006 - one place but sketched on two days and
directions. Monday, however - I daren't move an inch as buses, taxis and vans hurtle

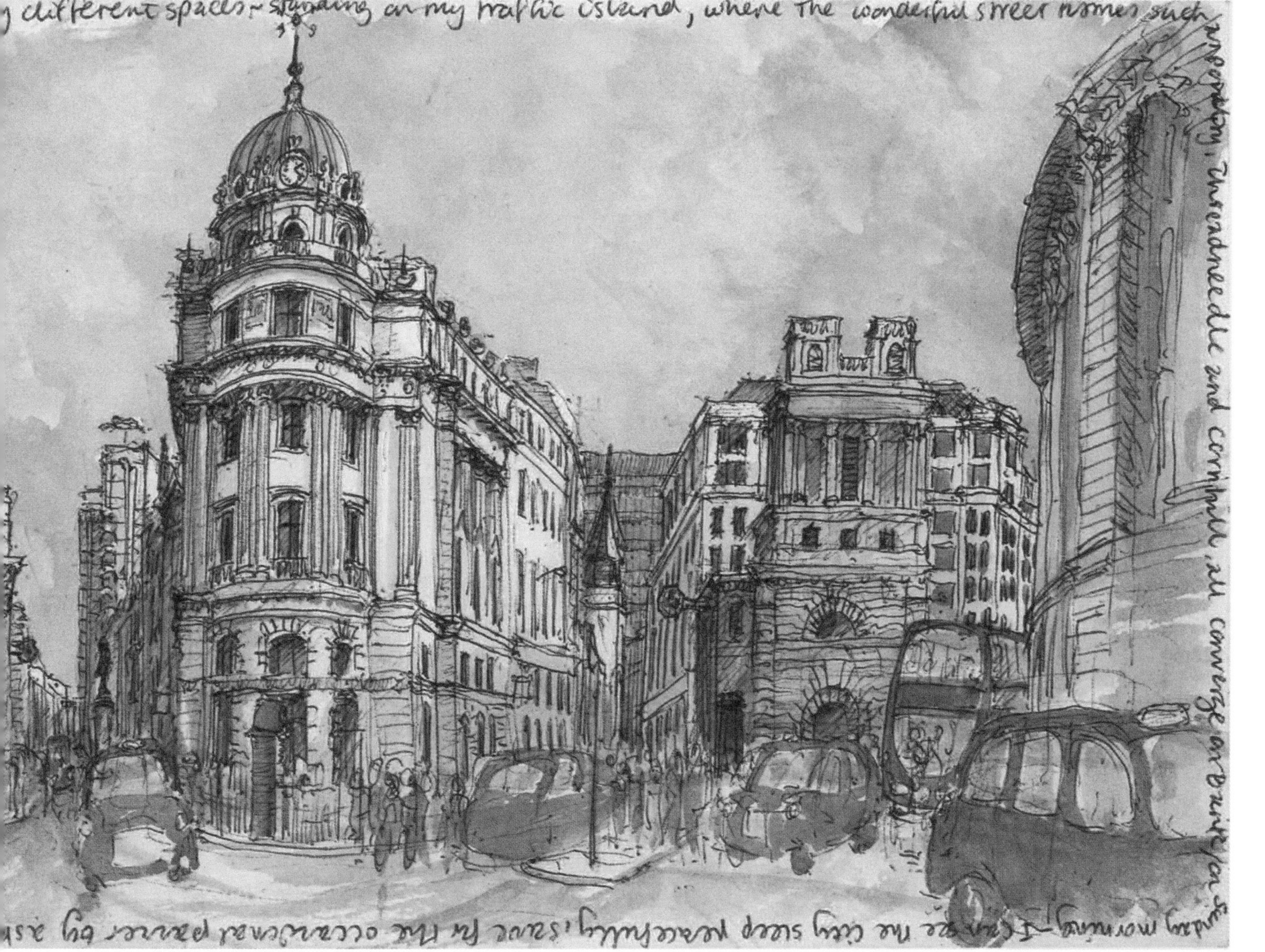
different spaces – standing on my traffic island, where the wonderful street names such
Threadneedle and Cornhill all converge on a
Sunday morning – I can see the city sleep peacefully, save for the occasional passer by as

Thursday 9th and Friday 10th February 2006 – several years ago, as part of the fab refur

up ... and the restaurant staff

are already preparing for another busy day ...

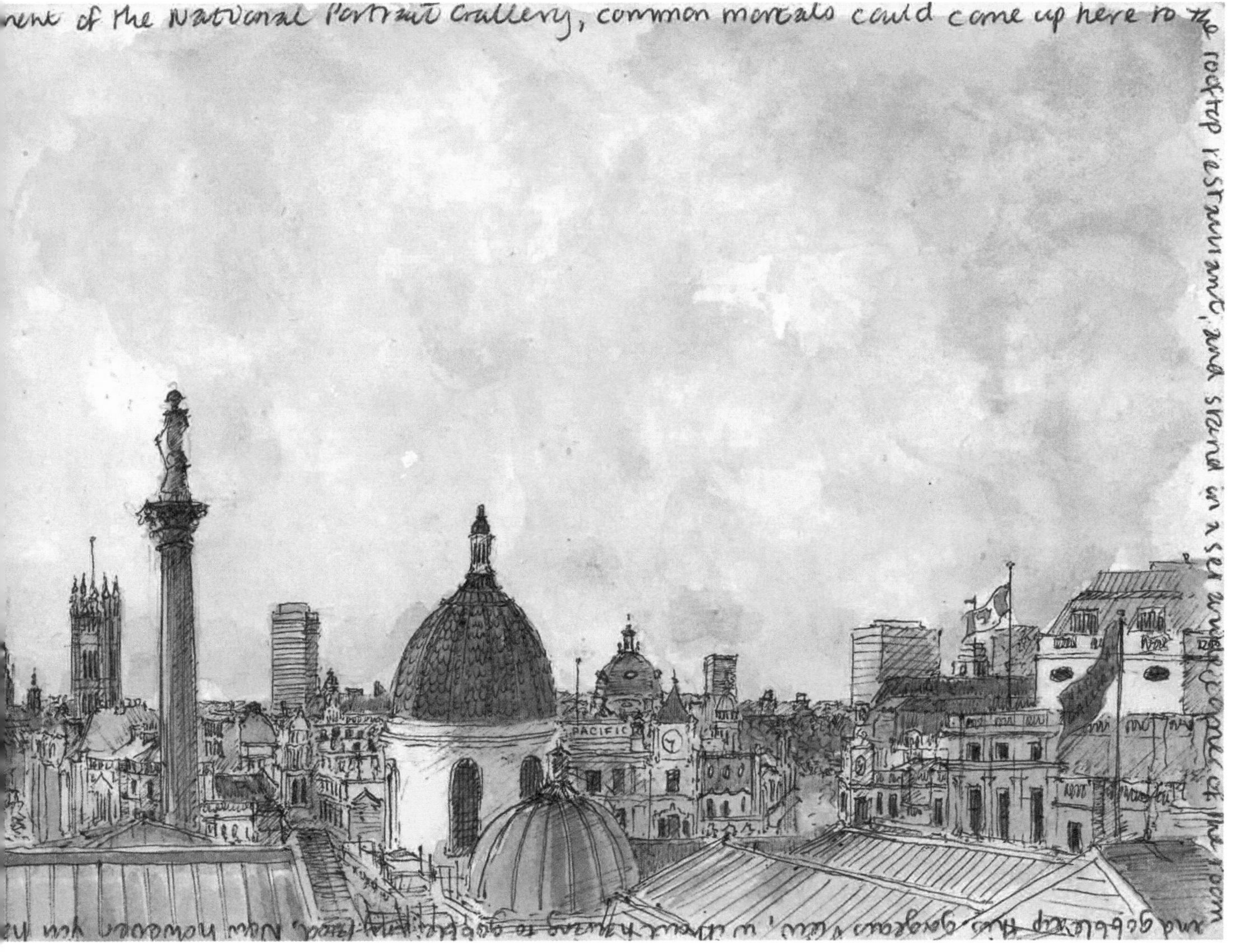
nent of the National Portrait Gallery, common mortals could come up here to the
rooftop restaurant, and stand in a
of the room
and gobble up this gorgeous view, without having to
food. Now however you ha
PACIFIC

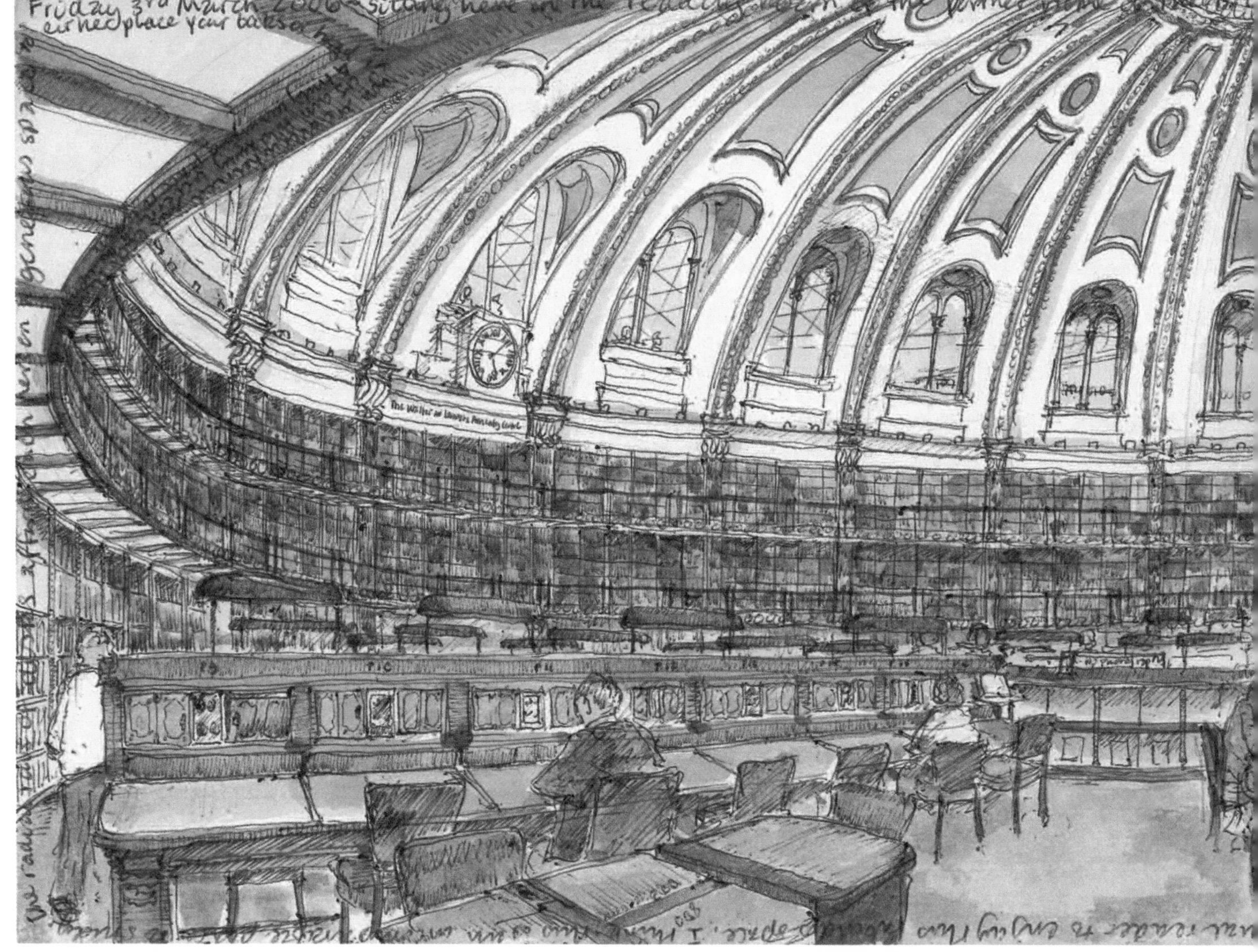

19

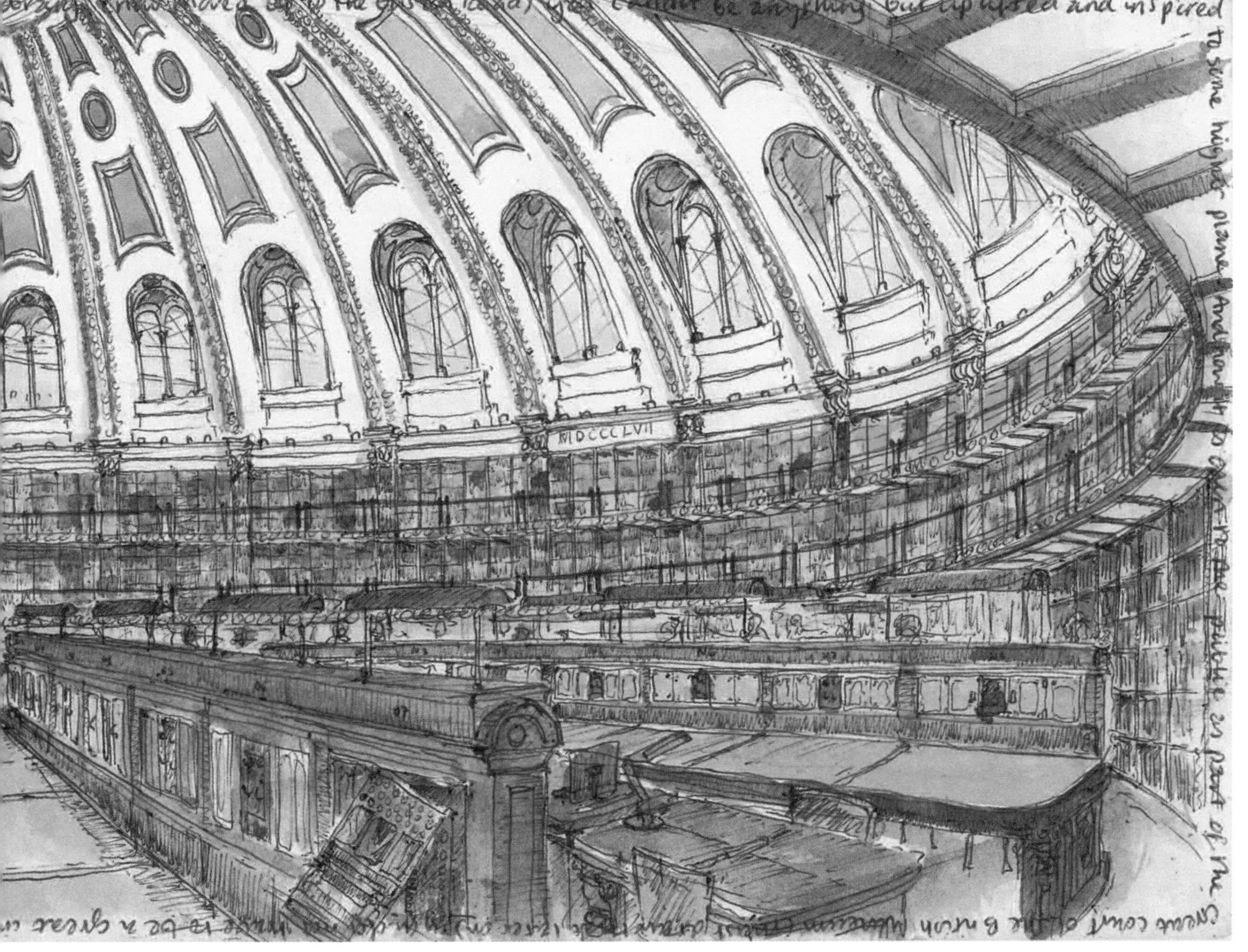

be anything but uplifted and inspired
to some higher plane
MDCCCLVII

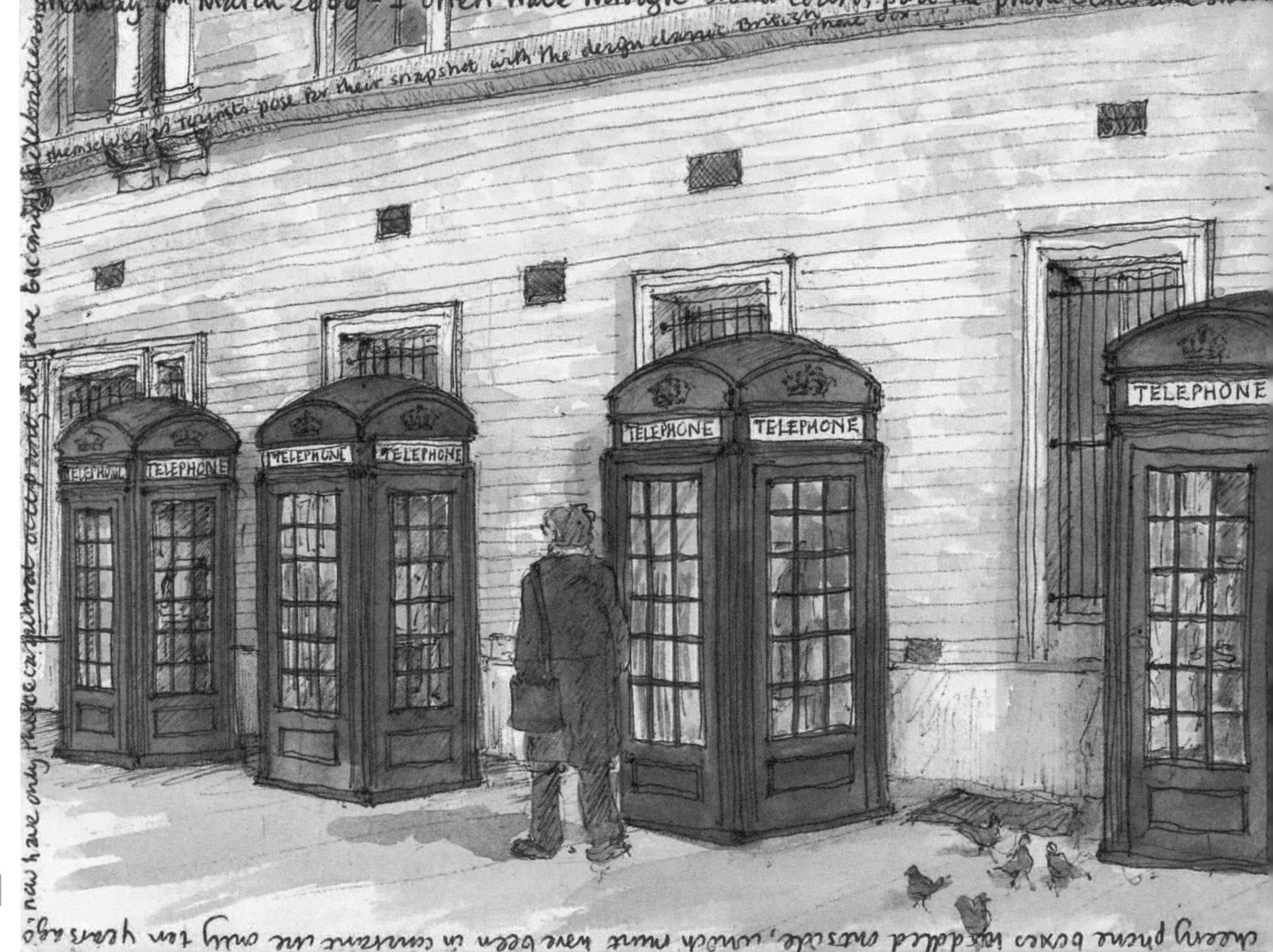
I often walk through Broad Court, past the phone boxes and
phone box.
tourists pose for their snapshot with the design classic British
cheery phone boxes huddled outside, which must have been in constant use only ten years ago.
TELEPHONE
TELEPHONE
TELEPHONE
TELEPHONE
TELEPHONE
TELEPHONE
TELEPHONE

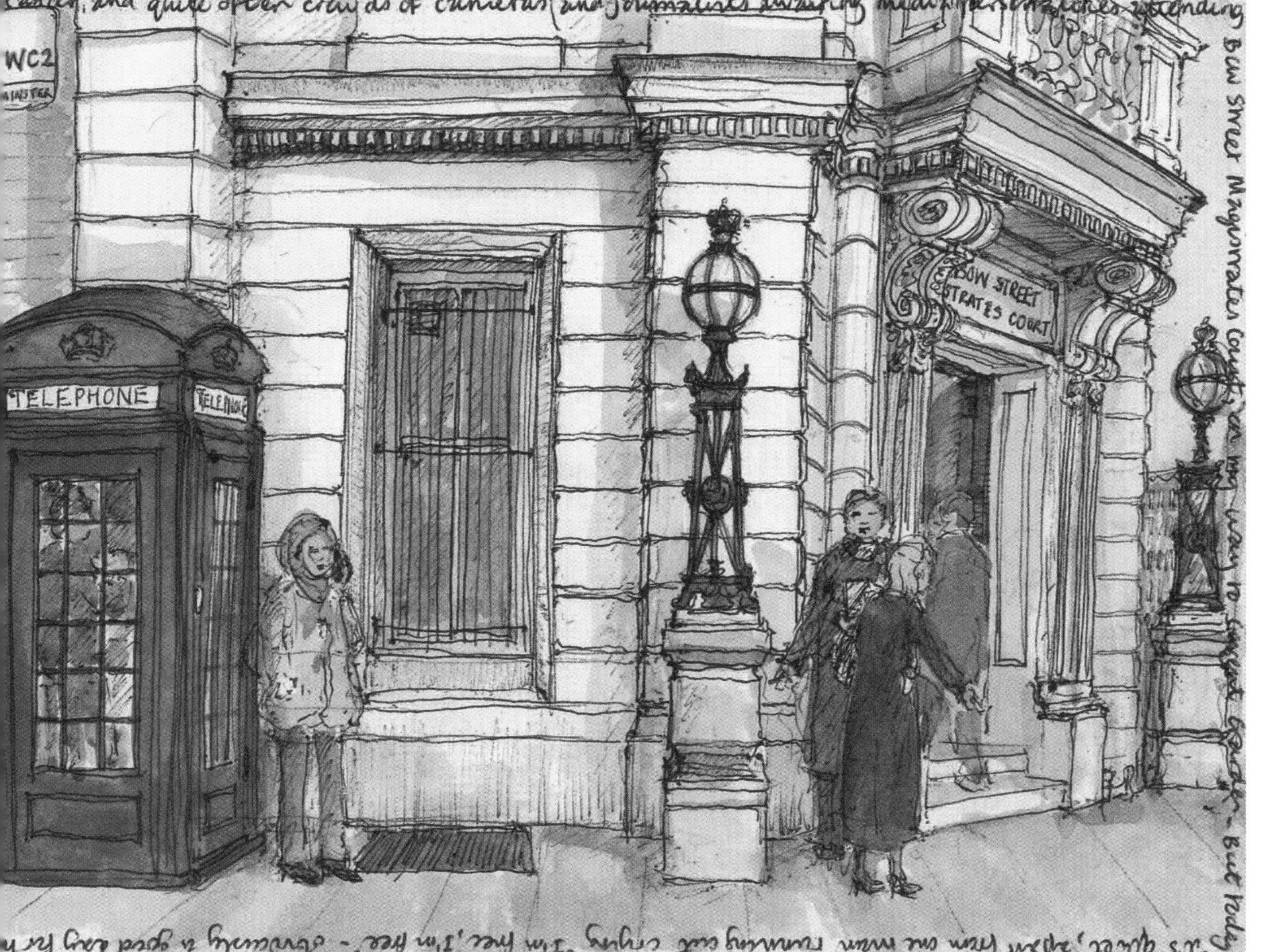
WC2
TELEPHONE
TELEPHONE
BOW STREET
STRATES COURT

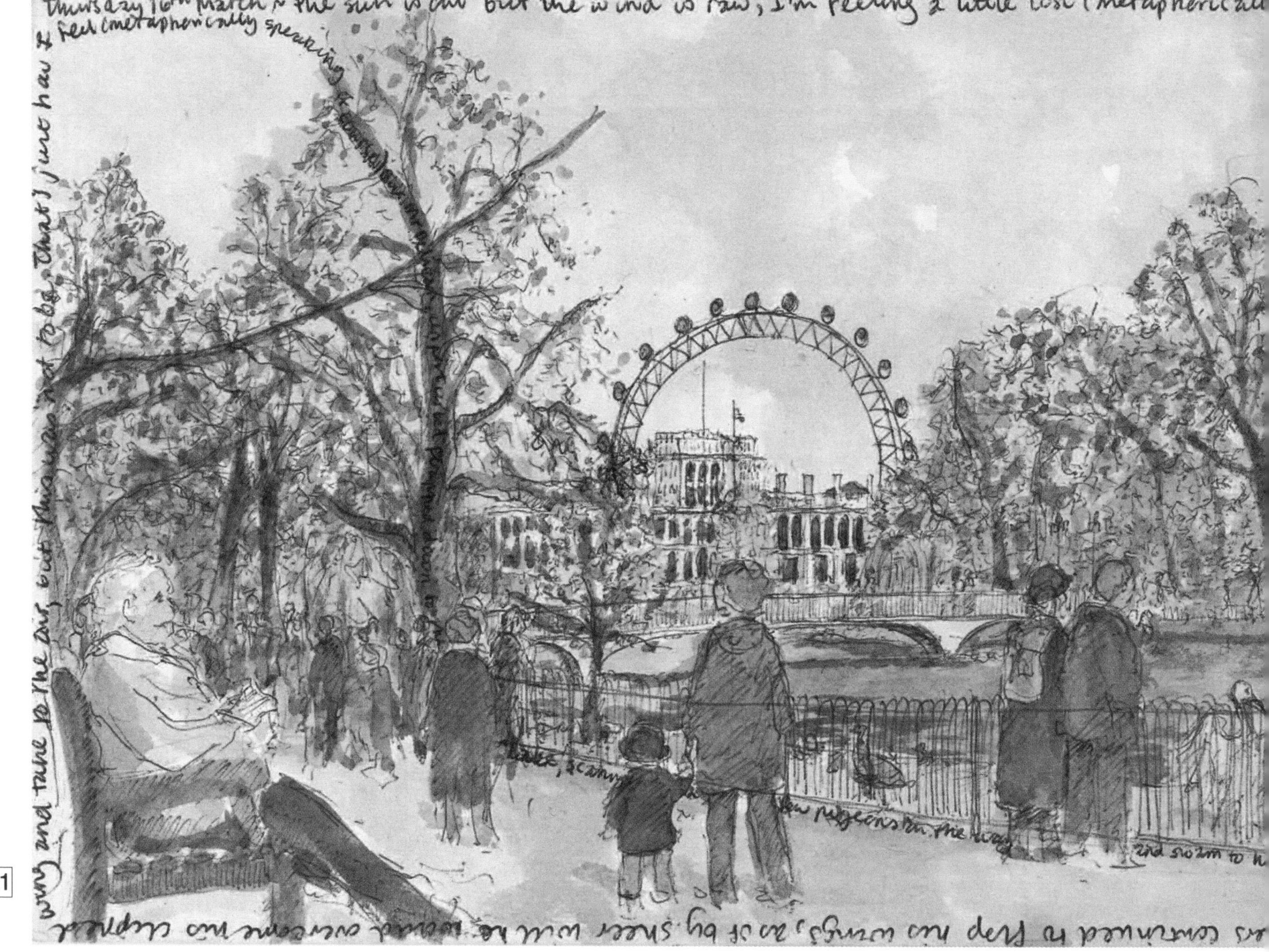

Thursday 16th March ~ the sun is out but the wind is raw, I'm feeling a little lost (metaphoricall
& feel (metaphorically speaking
and take to the air, but this was not to be, that I just hav
few pigeons in the way
and swam to h

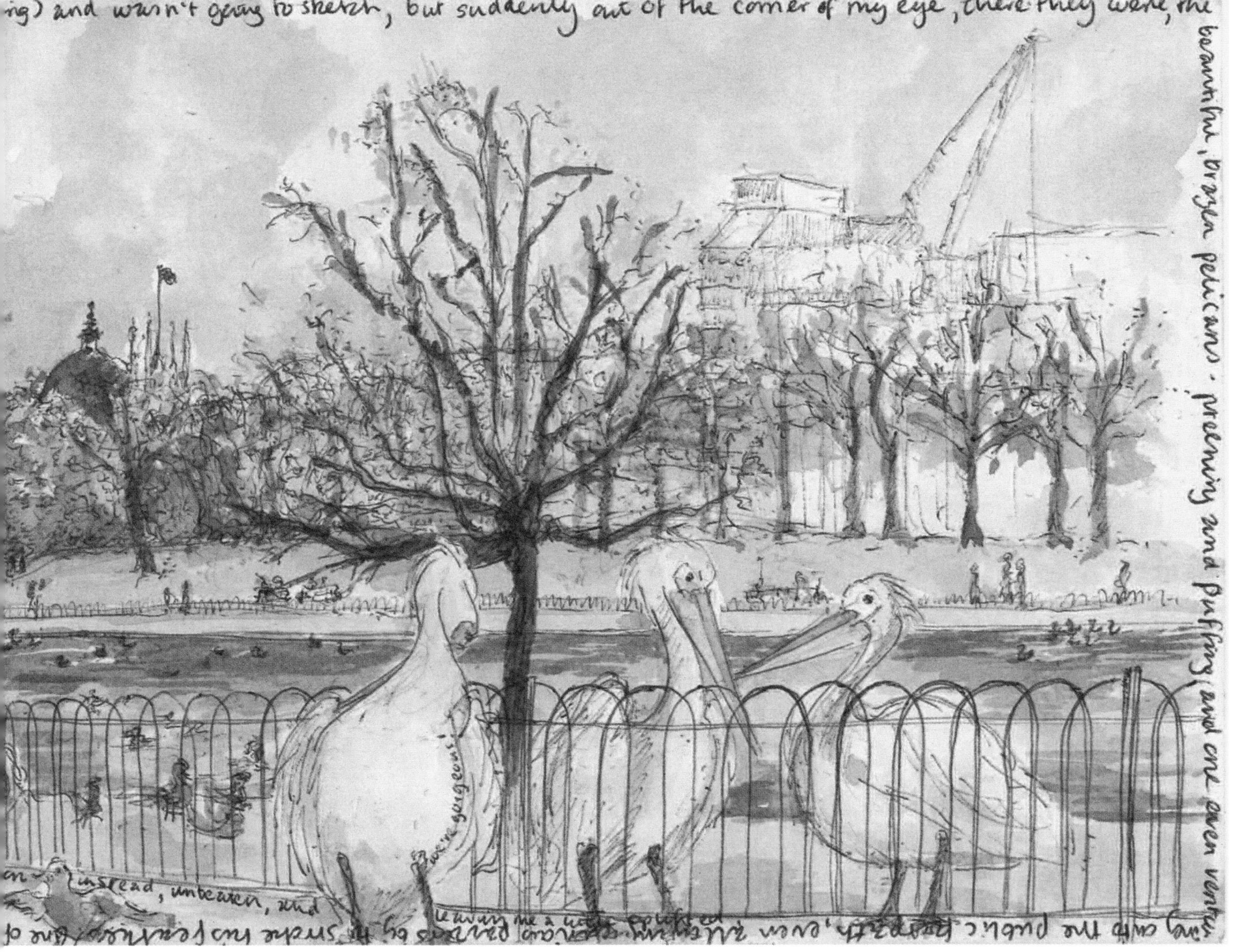
ing) and wasn't going to sketch, but suddenly out of the corner of my eye, there they were, the
beautiful, brazen pelicans - preening and puffing, and one even ventu
instead, uneaten, and
we're gorgeous

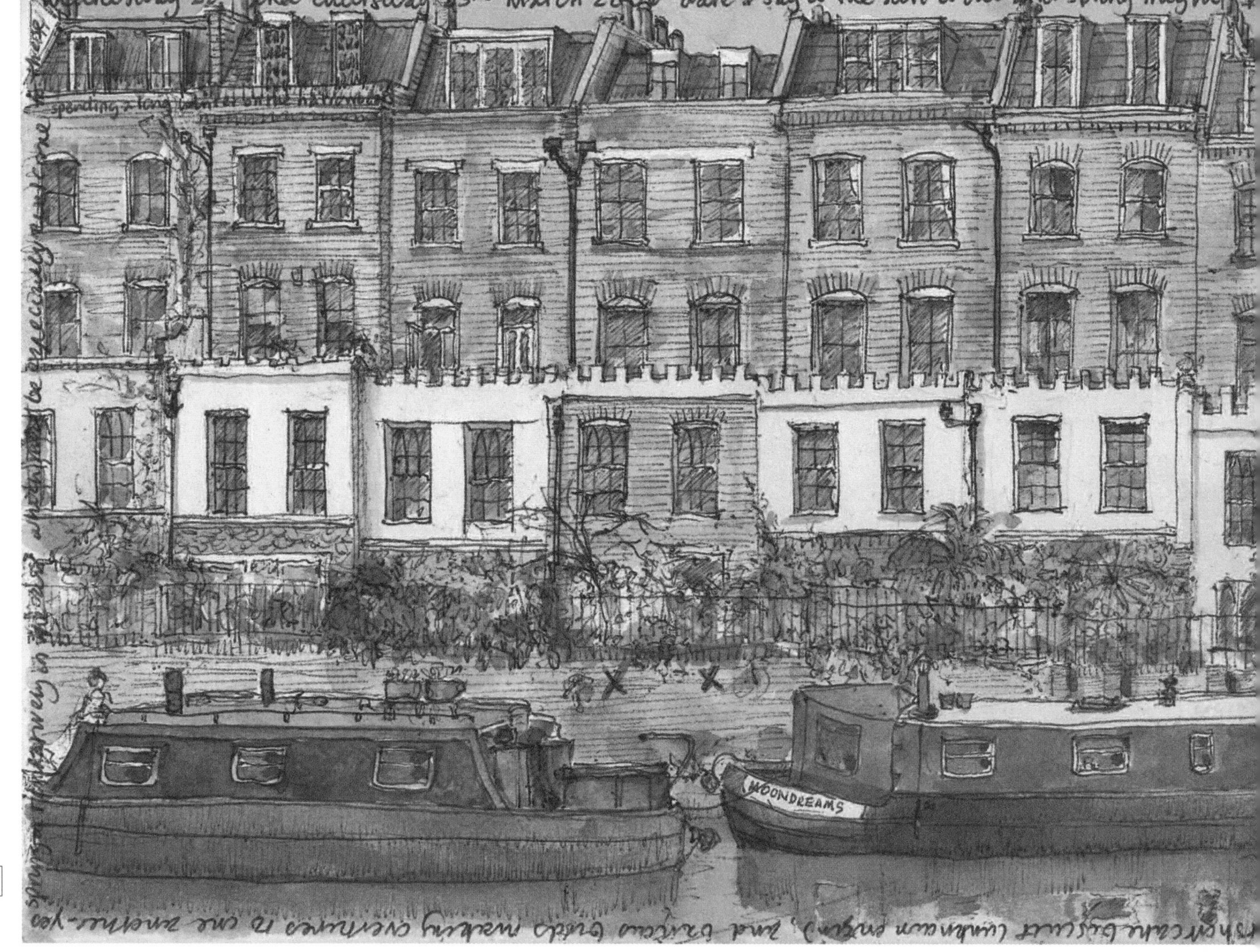
Wednesday 22nd and Thursday 23rd March 2006 - dare I say it the sun is out and spring might
MOONDREAMS

22

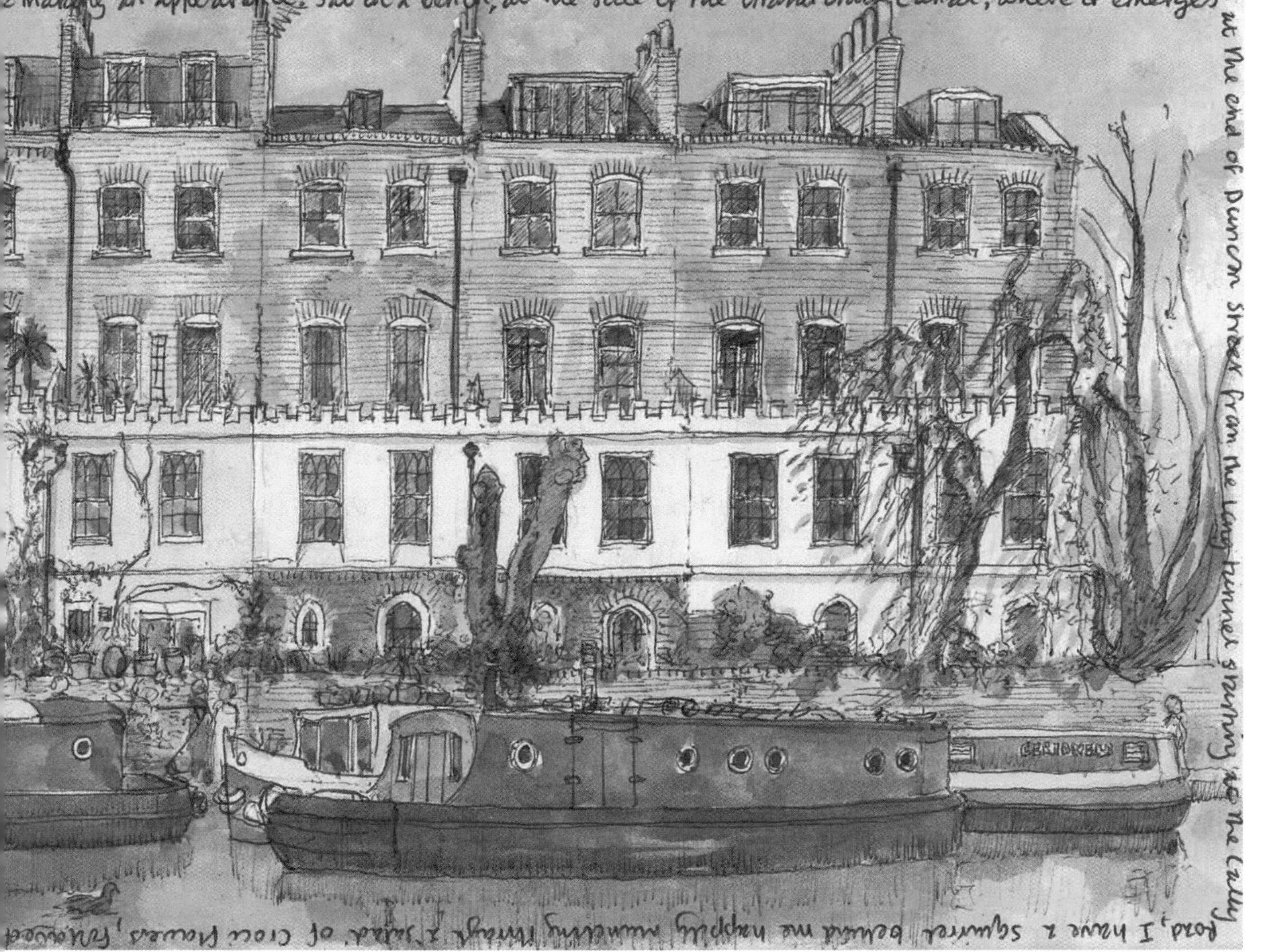
e making an appearance. Sat on a bench, at the side of the Grand Union Canal, where it emerges
at the end of Duncan Street from the long tunnel starting at the Cally
Road, I have a squirrel behind me happily munching through a salad of crocus flowers, followed

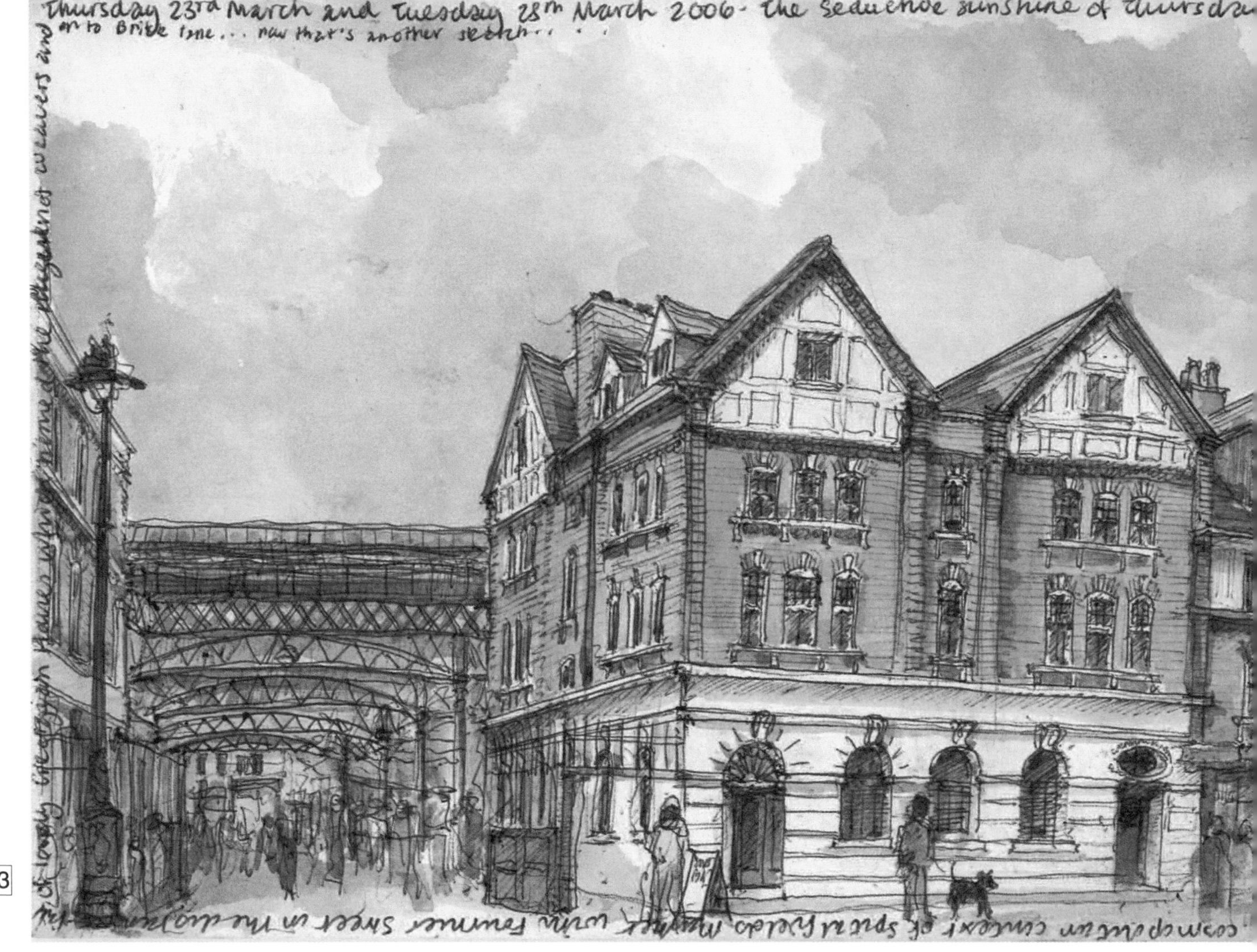
Thursday 23rd March and Tuesday 28th March 2006 - the seductive sunshine of Thursday
on to Brick Lane... now that's another sketch...

23

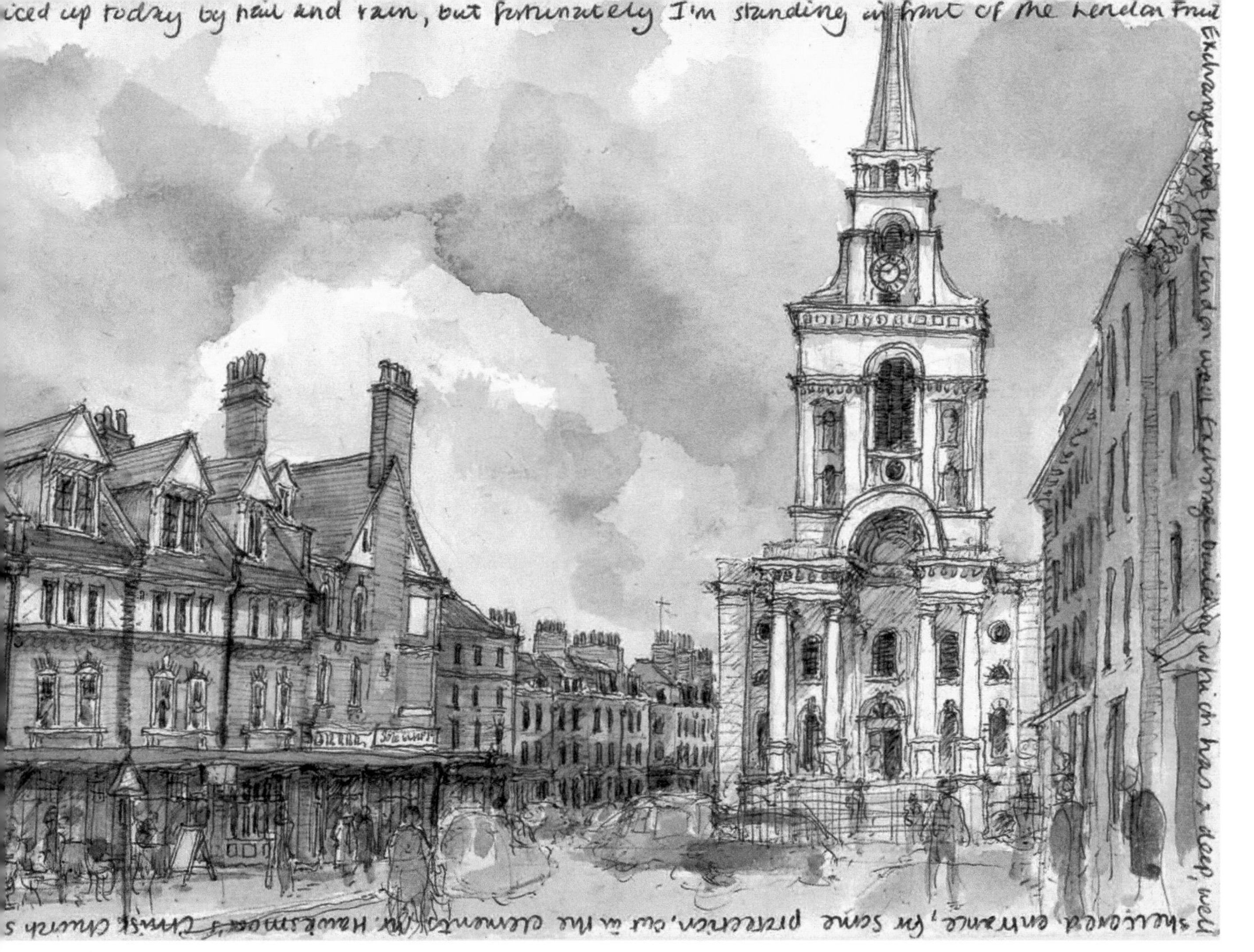
iced up today by hail and rain, but fortunately I'm standing in front of the London Fruit
Exchange
the London Wool Exchange building which has a deep, well
sheltered entrance, for some protection, out in the elements Mr. Hawksmoor's Christ Church's

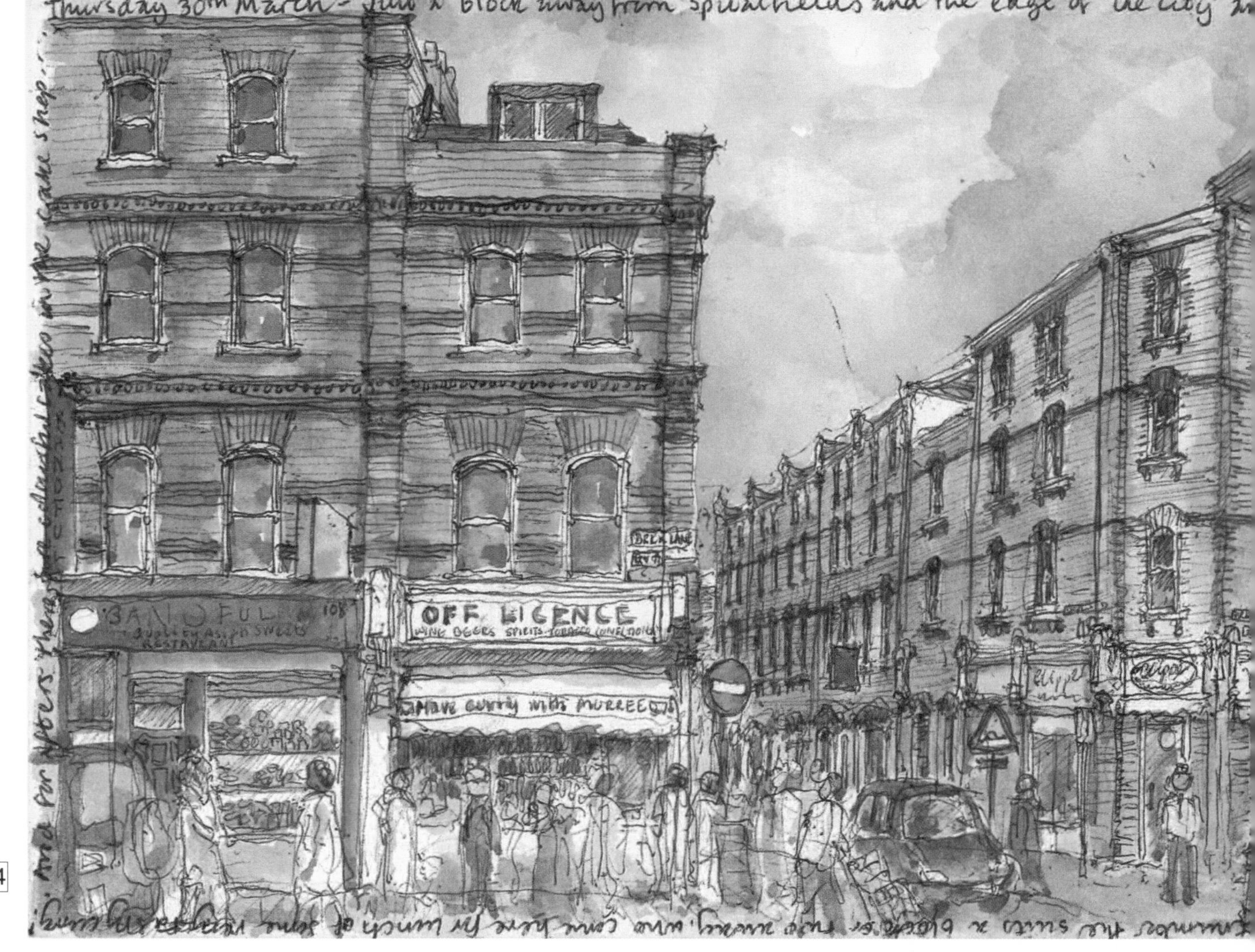
Thursday 30th March – Just a block away from Spitalfields and the edge of 'the City'
OFF LICENCE

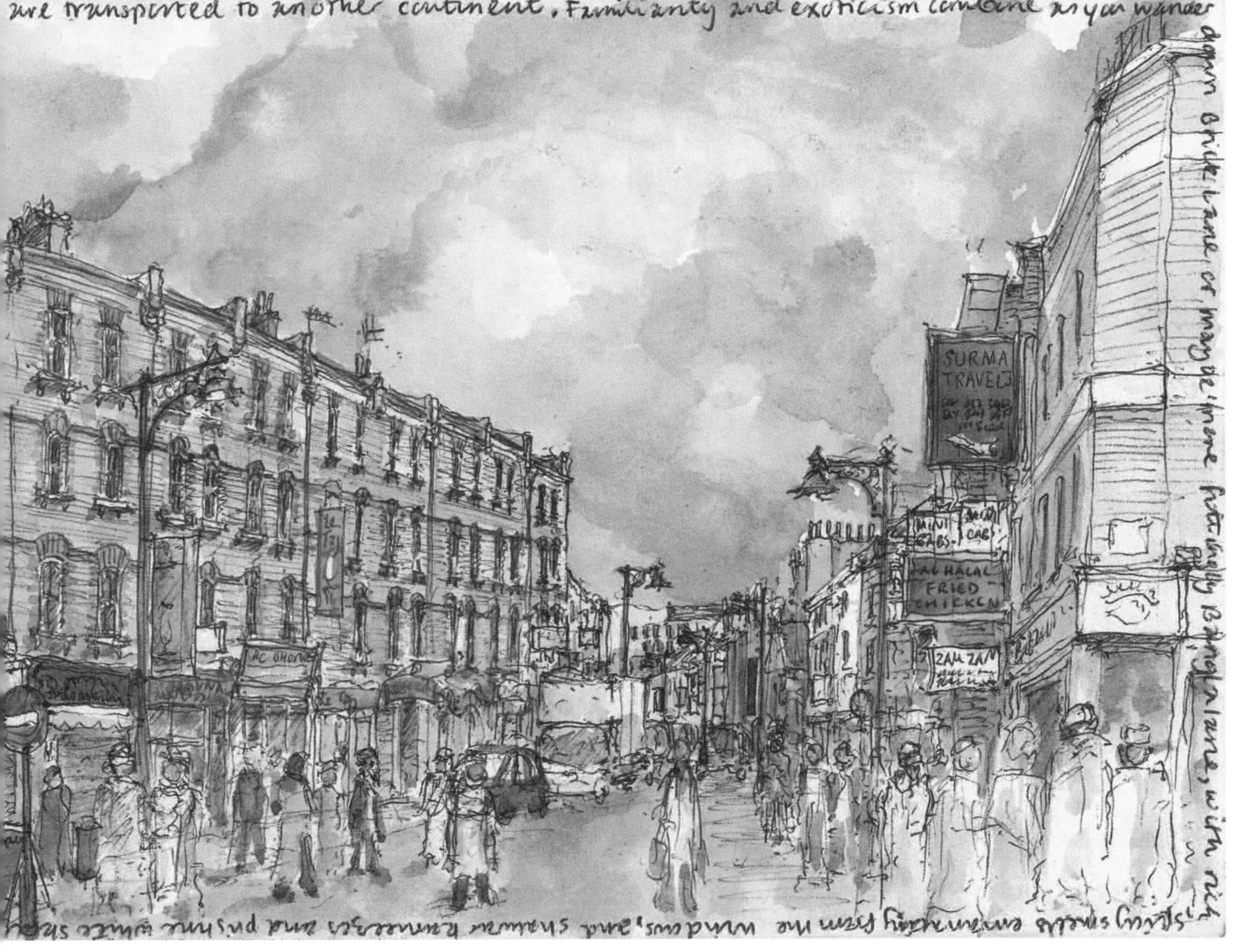
are transported to another continent. Familiarity and exoticism combine as you wander
down Brick Lane or maybe 'more fittingly Banglatown', with rich,
spicy smells emanating from the windows, and shalwar kameezes and pristine white skull
SURMA
TRAVELS
MINI
CABS
AL HALAL
FRIED
CHICKEN
ZAM ZAM

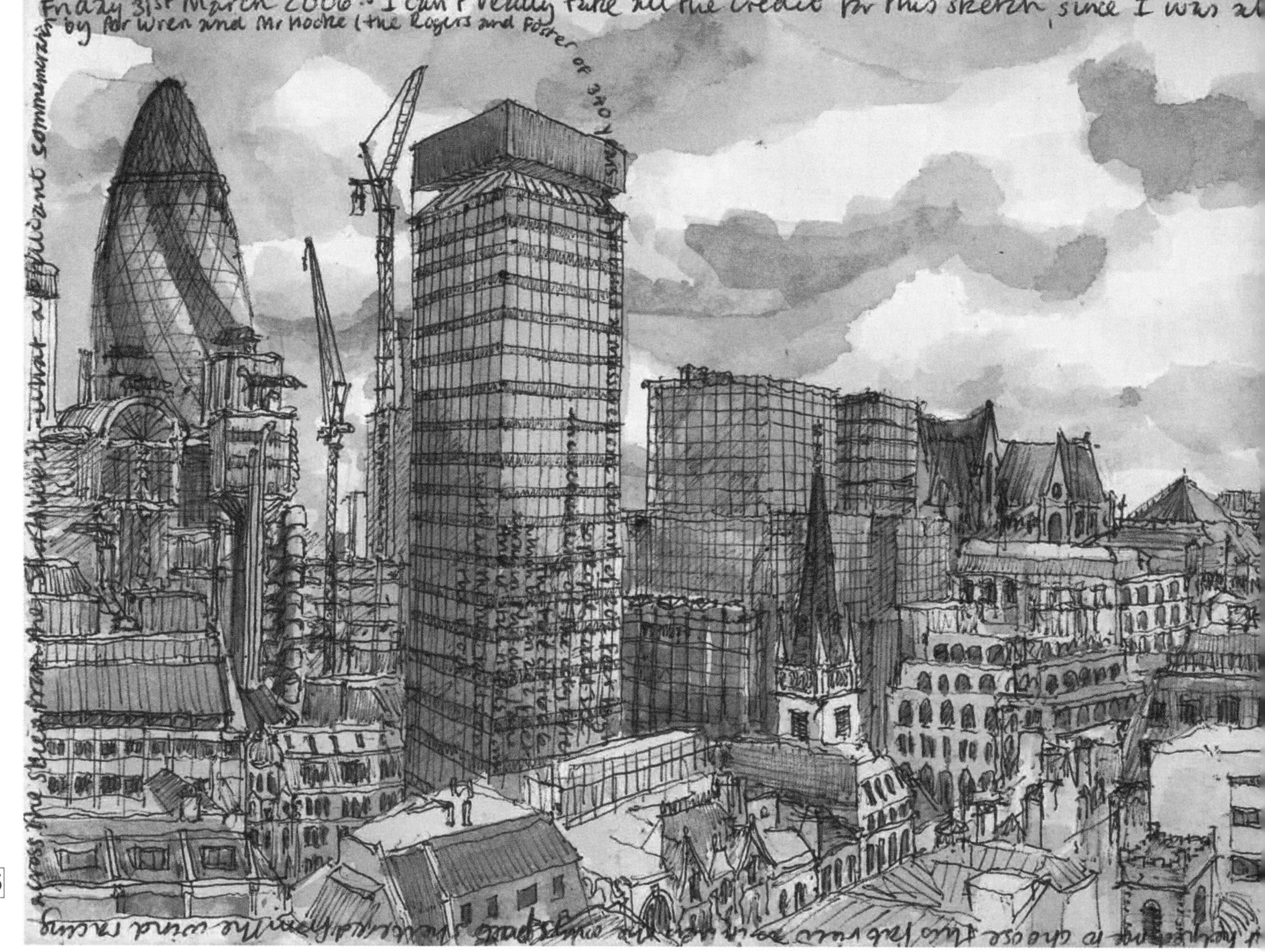
Friday 31st March 2006 – I can't really take all the credit for this sketch since I was

25

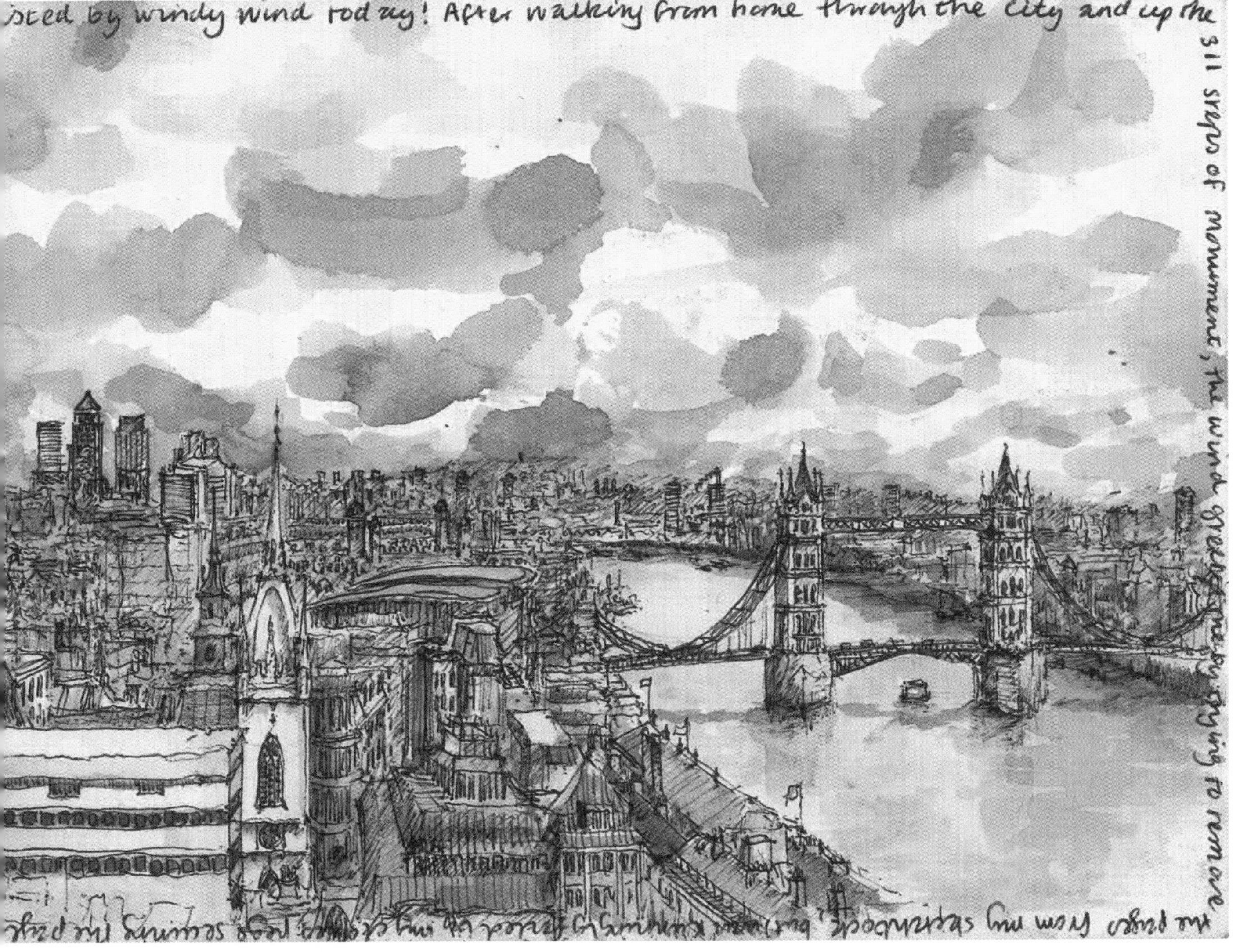
isted by windy wind today! After walking from home through the city and up the
311 steps of Monument, the wind greeted me by trying to remove

26

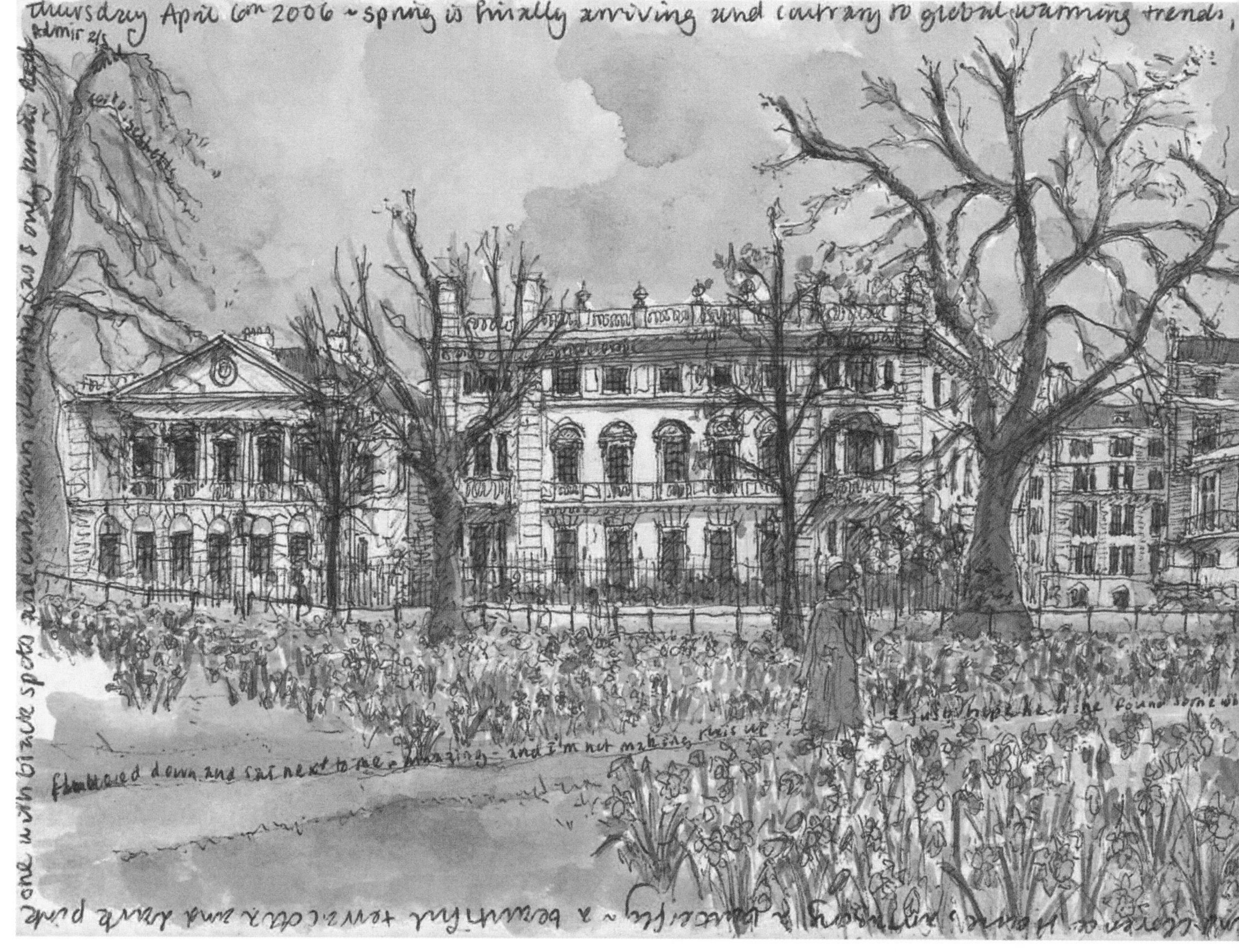
Thursday April 6th 2006 ~ spring is finally arriving and contrary to global warming trends,
and I'm not making this up

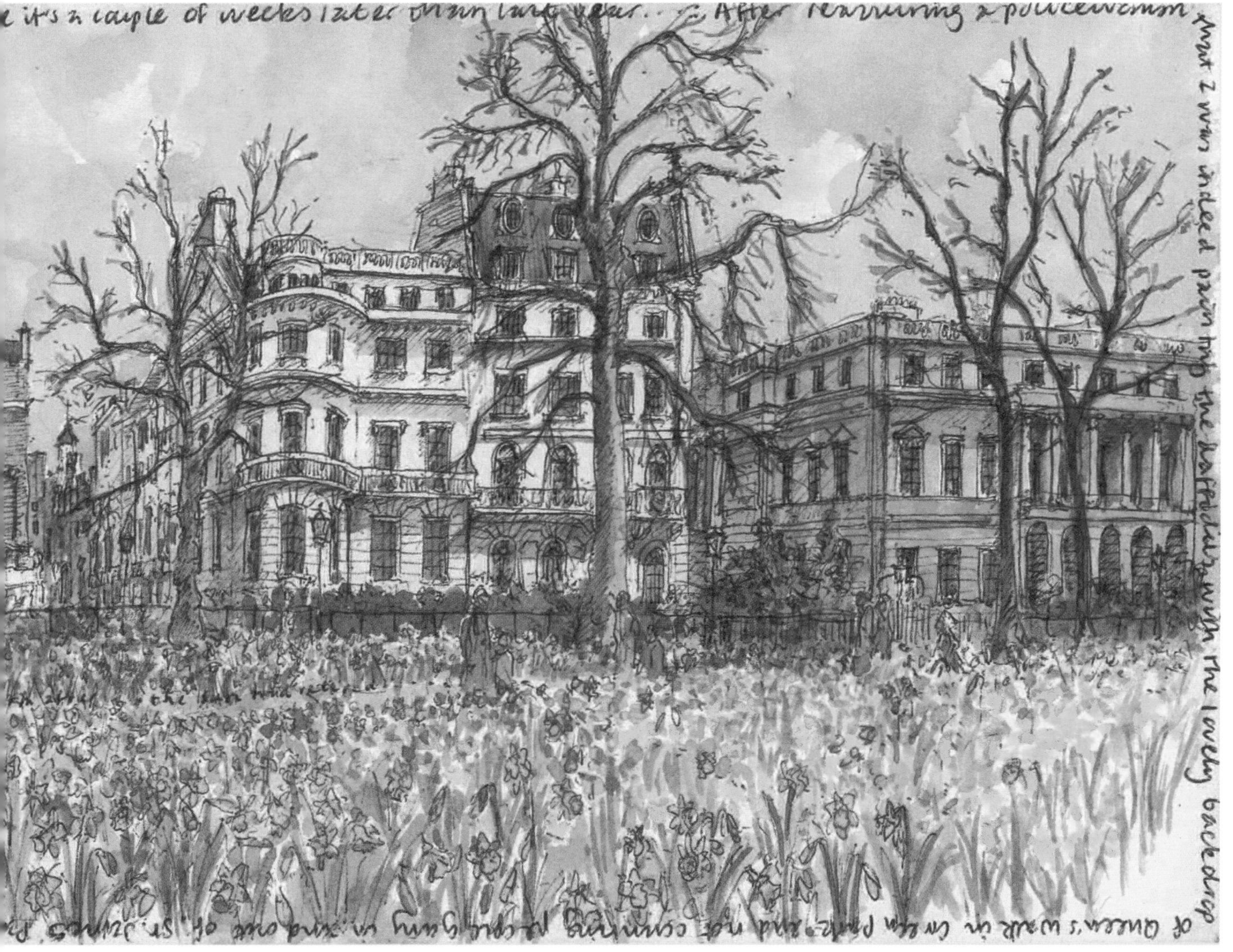
it's a couple of weeks later than last year. .. After reassuring a policewoman
that I was indeed painting the daffodils with the lovely backdrop

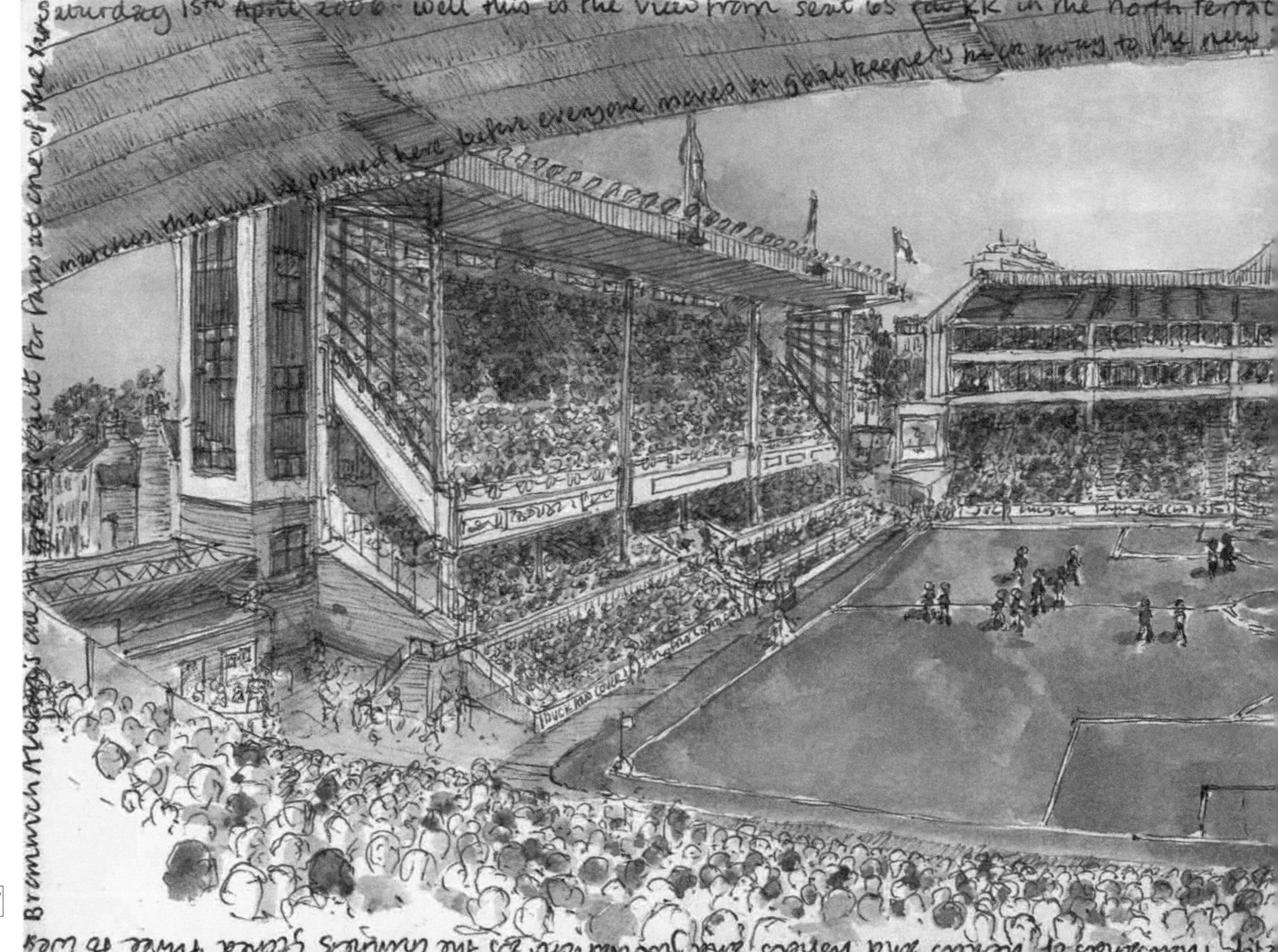
Saturday 15th April 2006 - well this is the view from seat 65 row KK in the North Terrac
matches that will be played here before everyone moves to
of thousands of heads and hands applaud and jubilations as the Canaries scored three to West

27

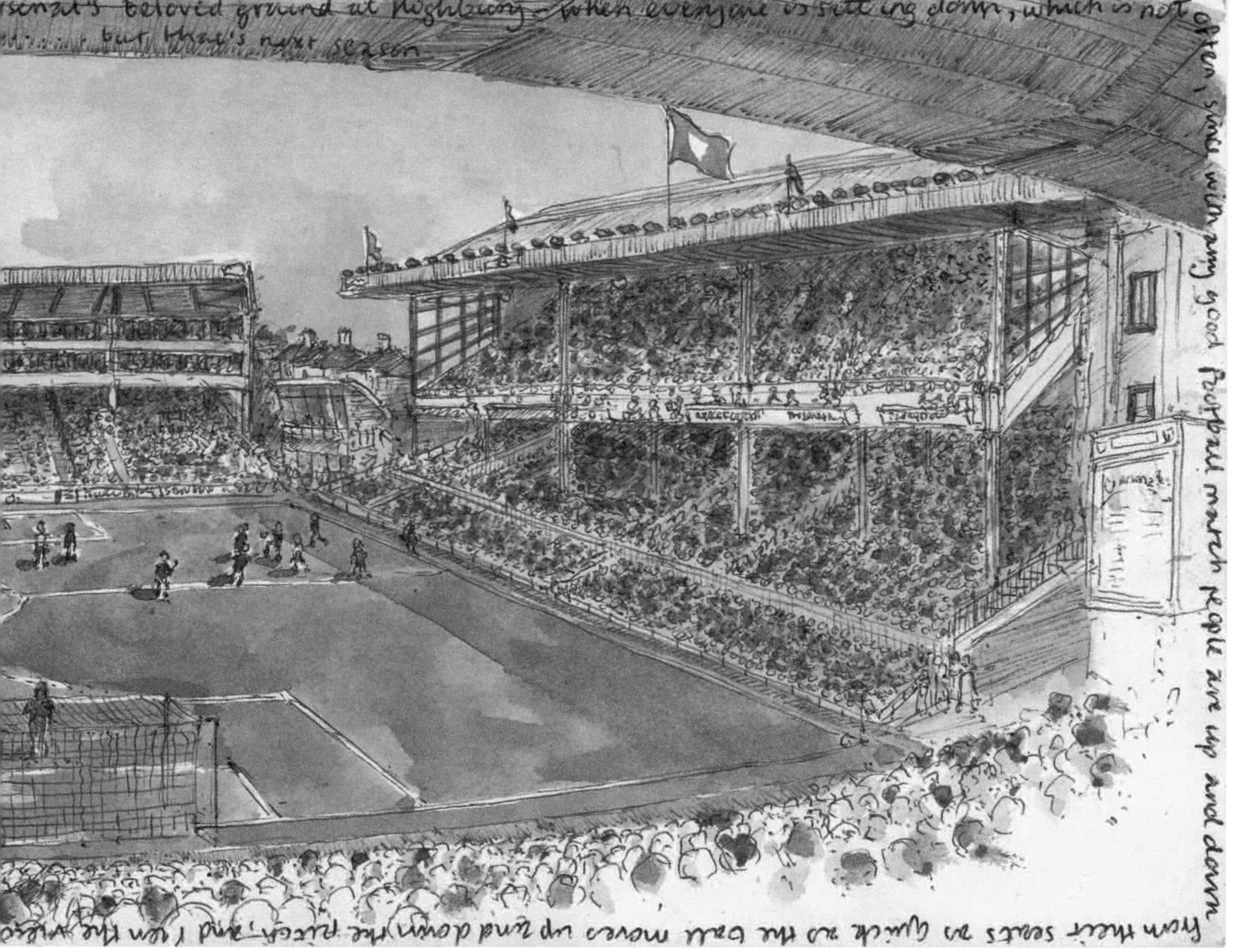
beloved ground at Highbury - when everyone is sitting down, which is not
but that's next season
often, since with any good football match people are up and down
from their seats as quick as the ball moves up and down the pitch, and then

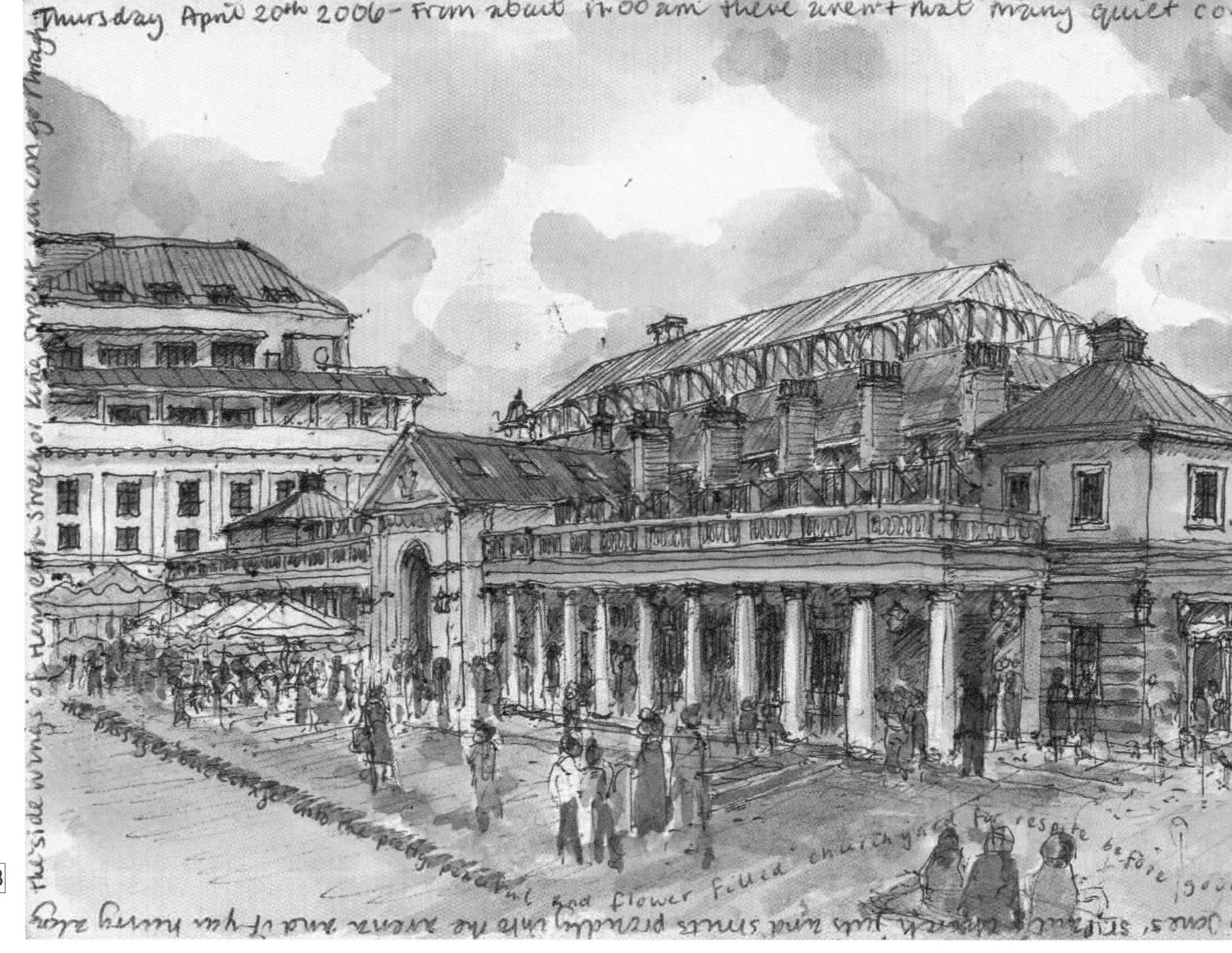
Thursday April 20th 2006 - From about 11.00 am there weren't that many quiet co
the passages converge into the pretty peaceful and flower filled churchyard for respite before going

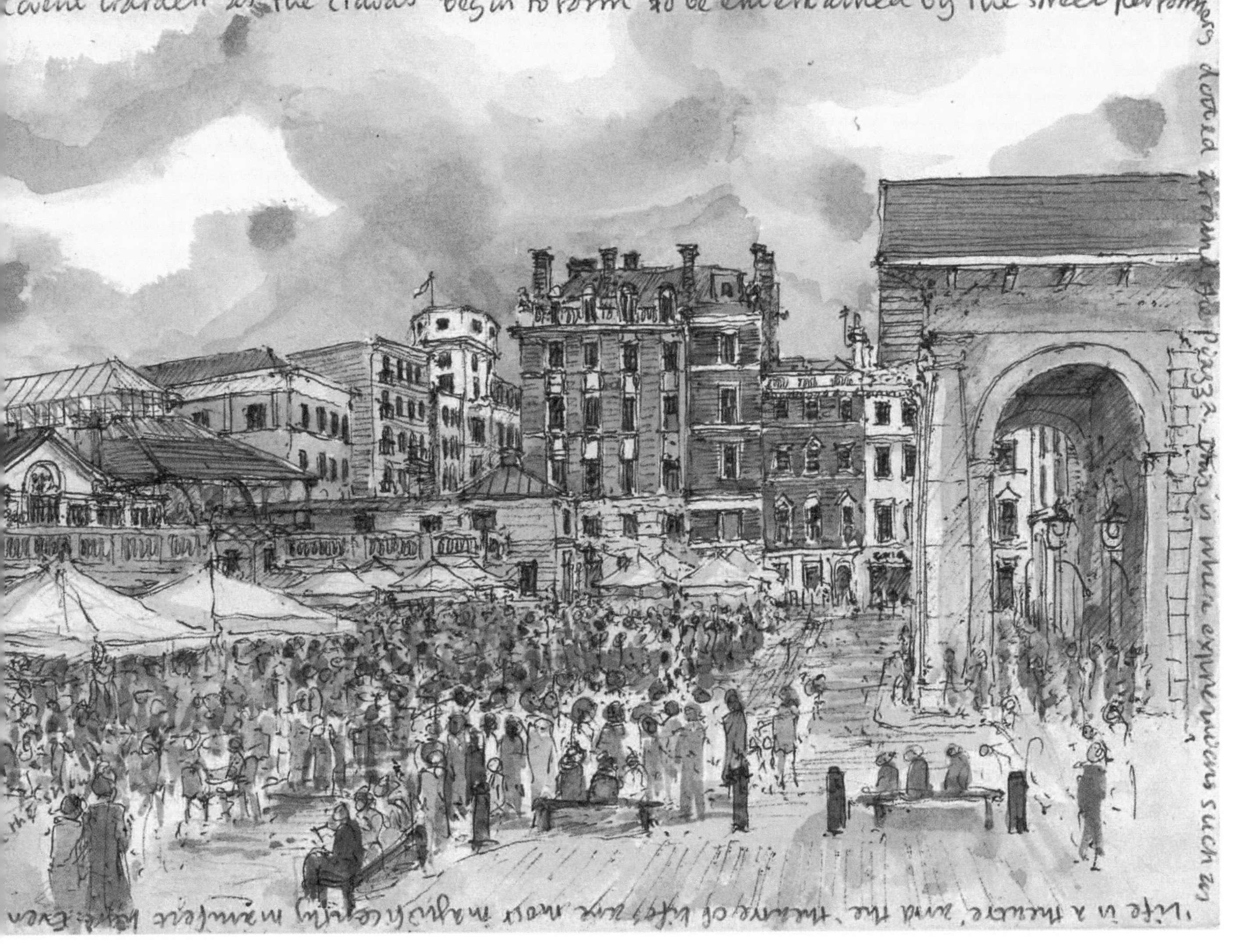
Covent Garden as the crowds begin to form to be entertained by the street performers
dotted around the Piazza. This is where expressions such as
'Life is a theatre' and the 'theatre of life' are most magnificently manifest here. Even

29

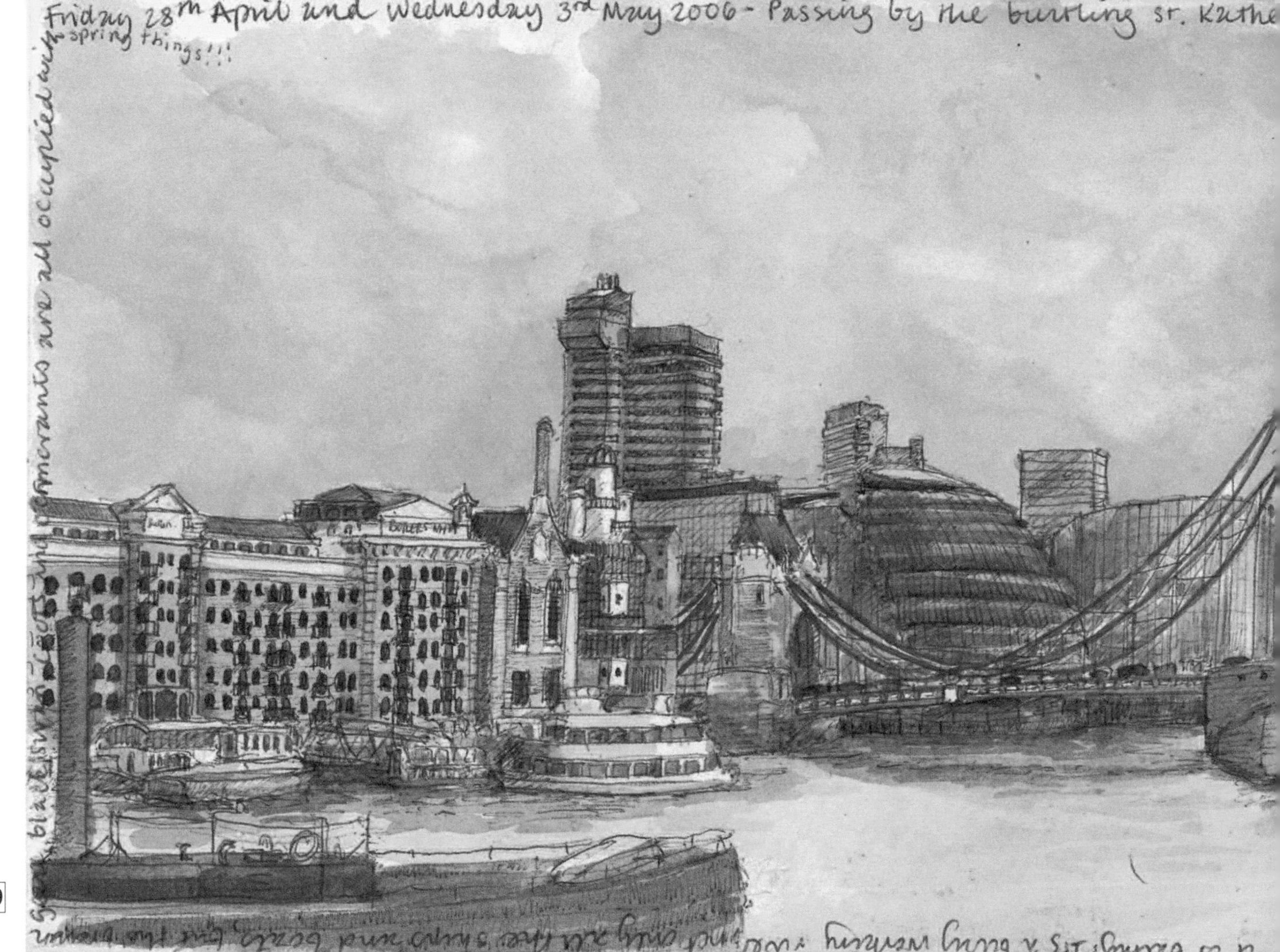
Friday 28th April and Wednesday 3rd May 2006 - Passing by the bustling St. Kathe
spring things!!!

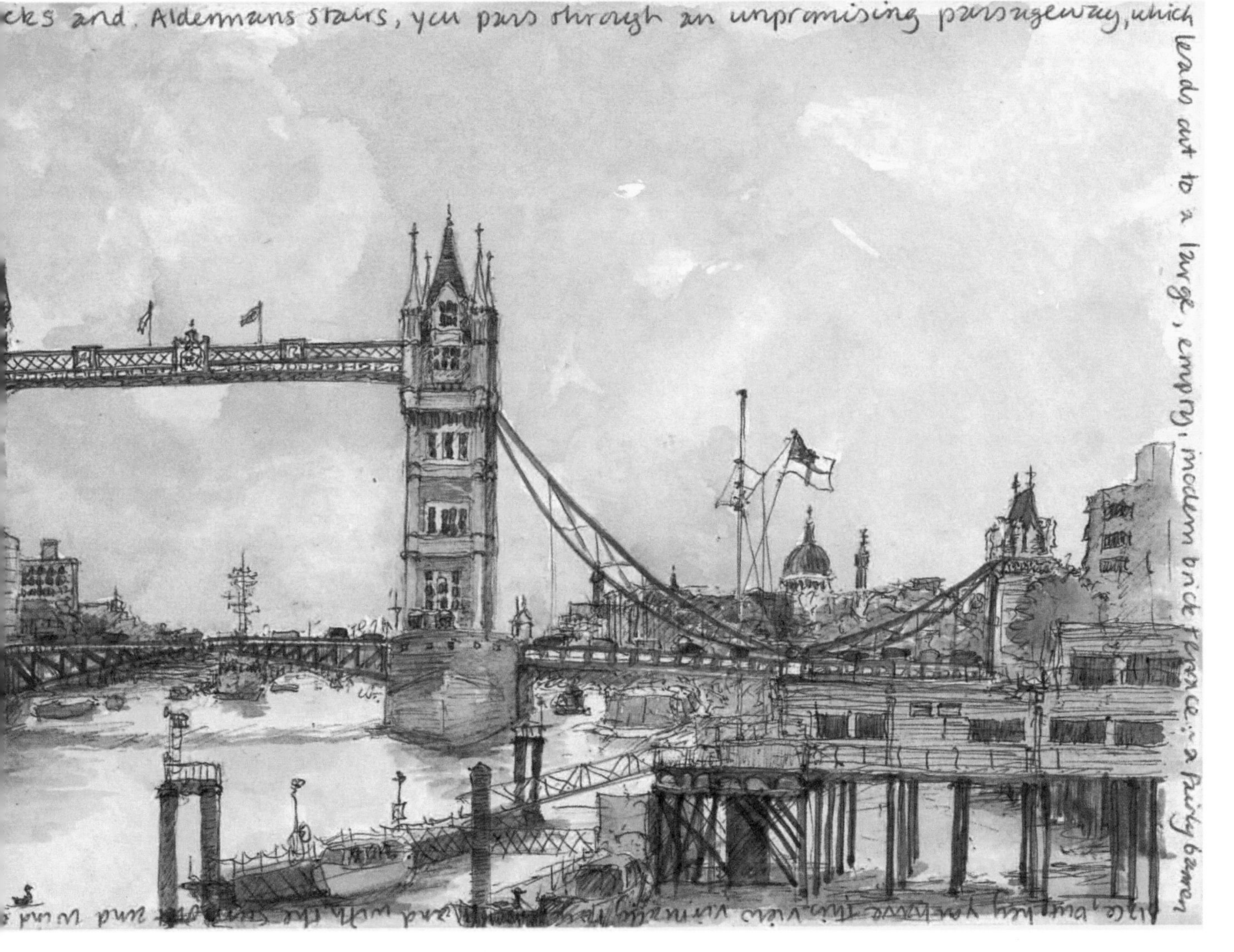
cks and Aldermans stairs, you pass through an unpromising passageway, which
leads out to a large, empty, modern brick terrace: a fairly barren

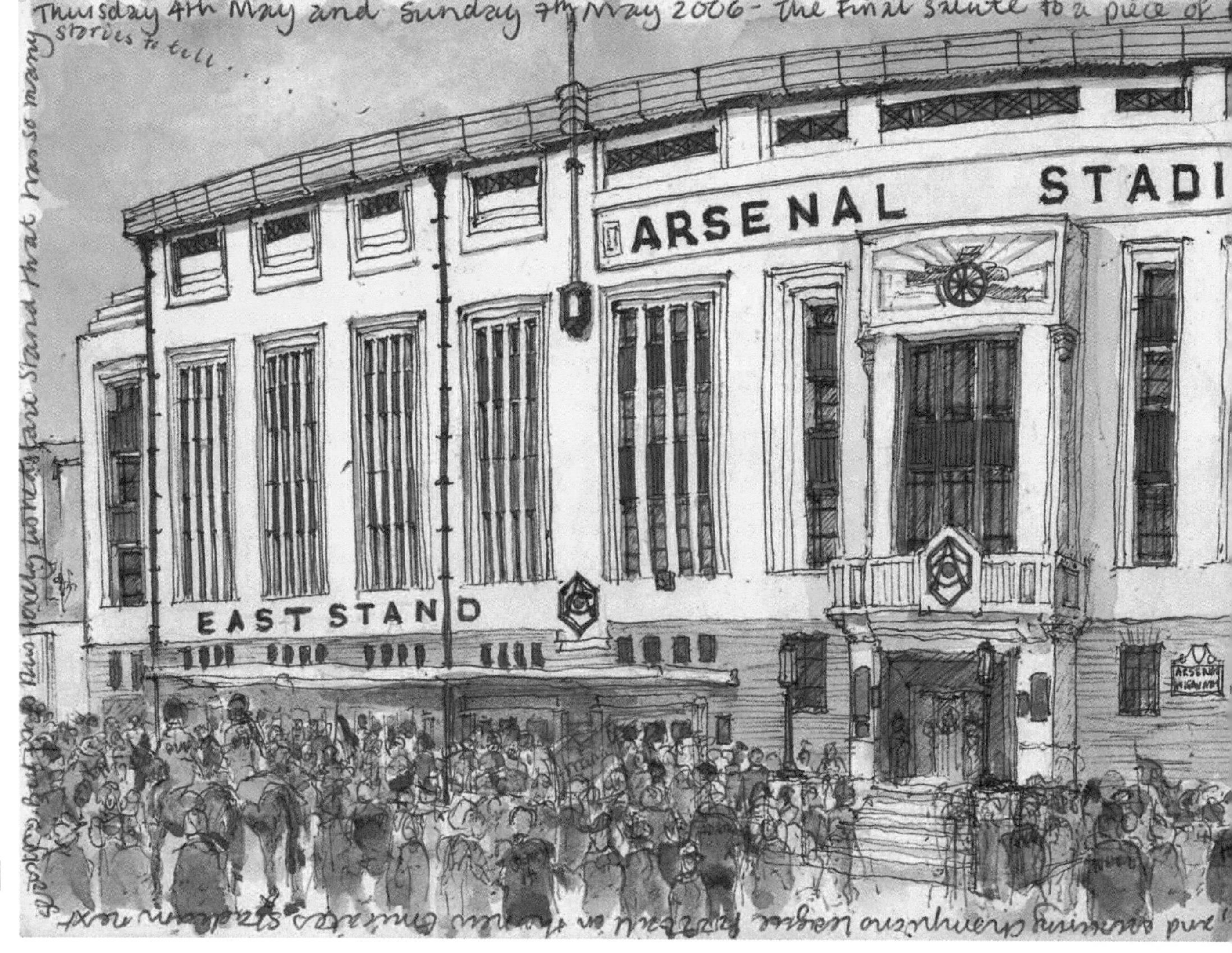
Thursday 4th May and Sunday 7th May 2006 - the final salute to a piece of
East Stand that has so many stories to tell . . .
ARSENAL STADI
EAST STAND

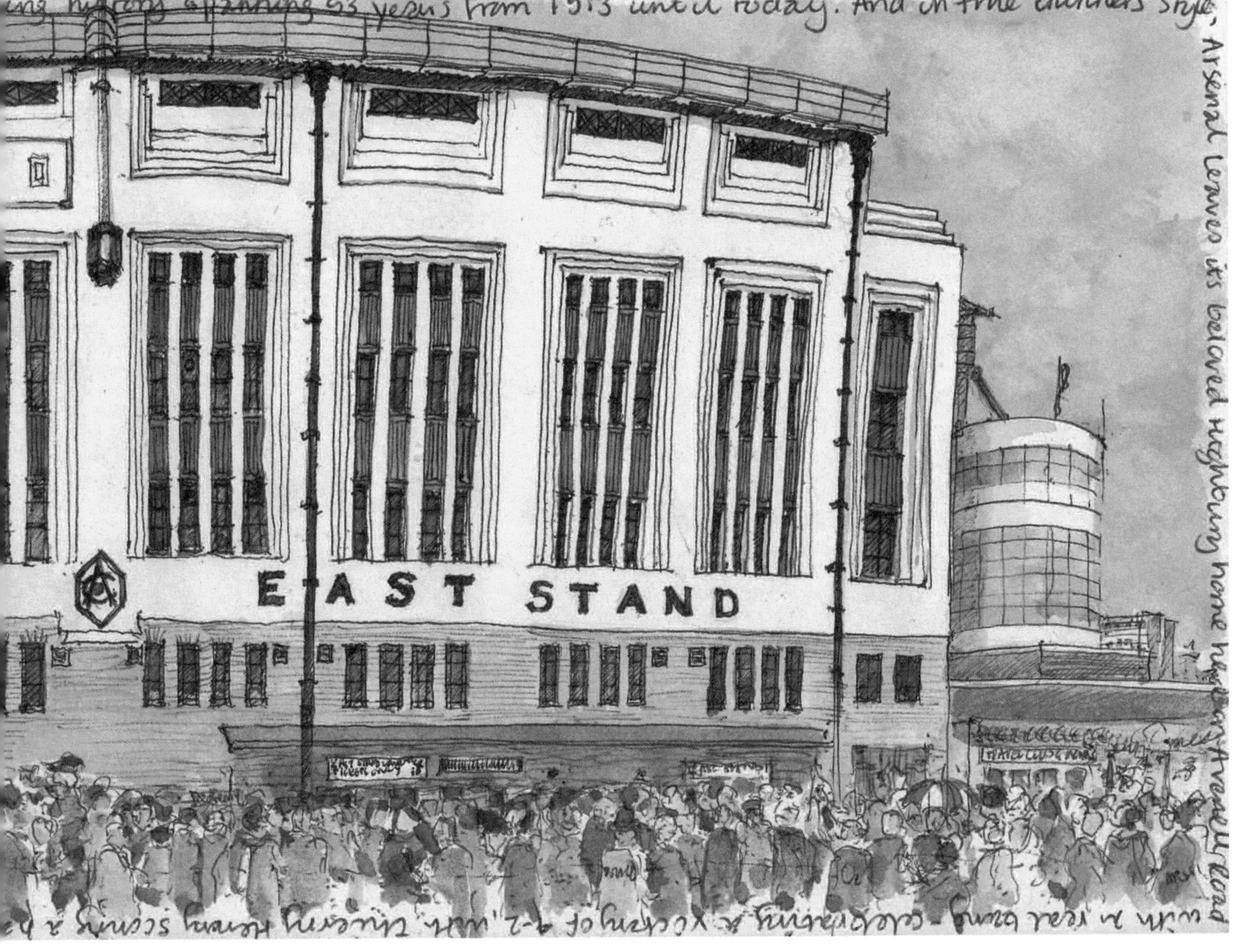
ing history spanning 93 years from 1913 until today. And in true Gunners style,
Arsenal leaves its beloved Highbury home in Avenell Road
with a real bang - celebrating a victory of 4-2 with Thierry Henry scoring
EAST STAND

31

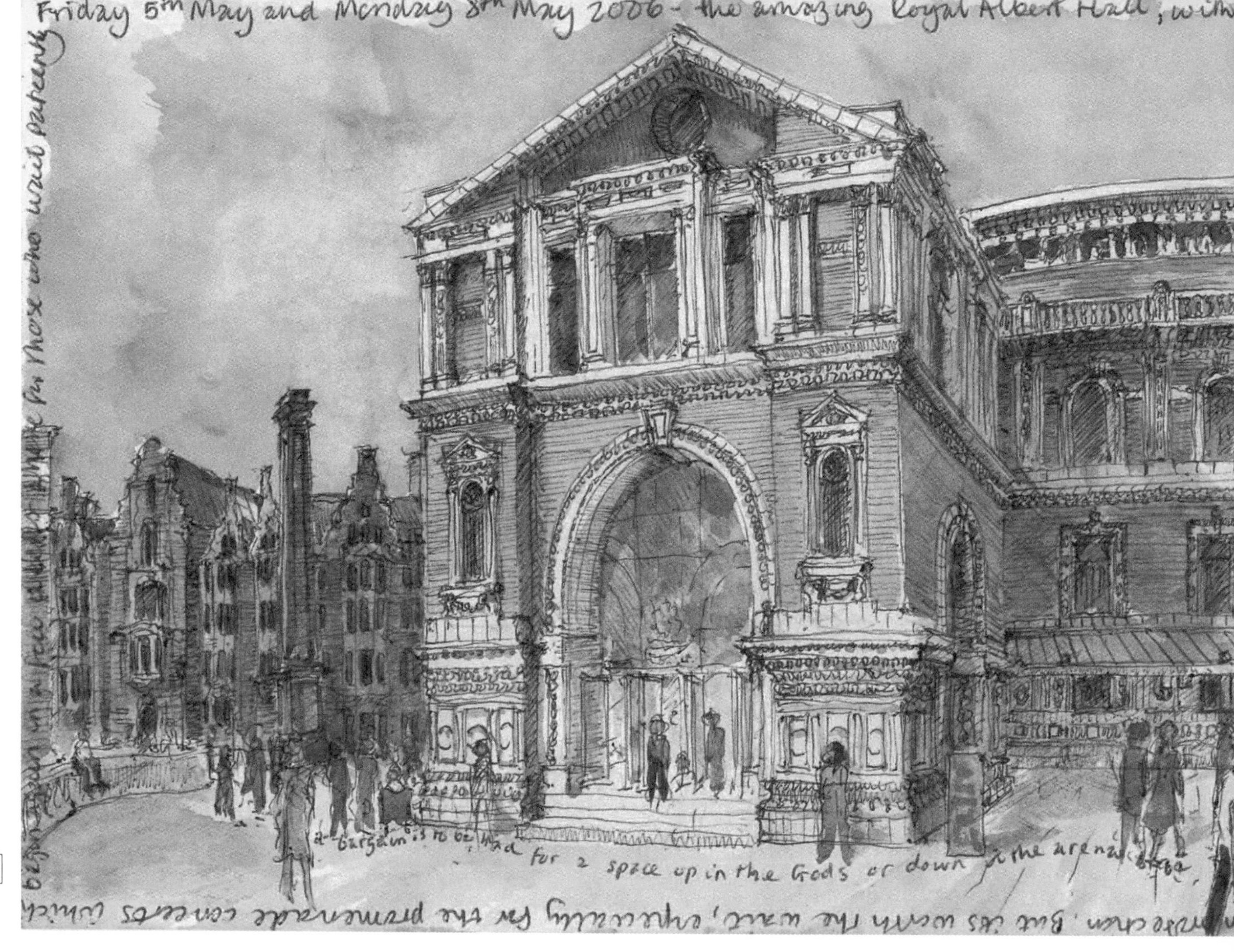
Friday 5th May and Monday 8th May 2006 - the amazing Royal Albert Hall, with
here for those who wait patiently
a bargain is to be had for a space up in the Gods or down in the arena area
so often. But it's worth the wait, especially for the promenade concerts which

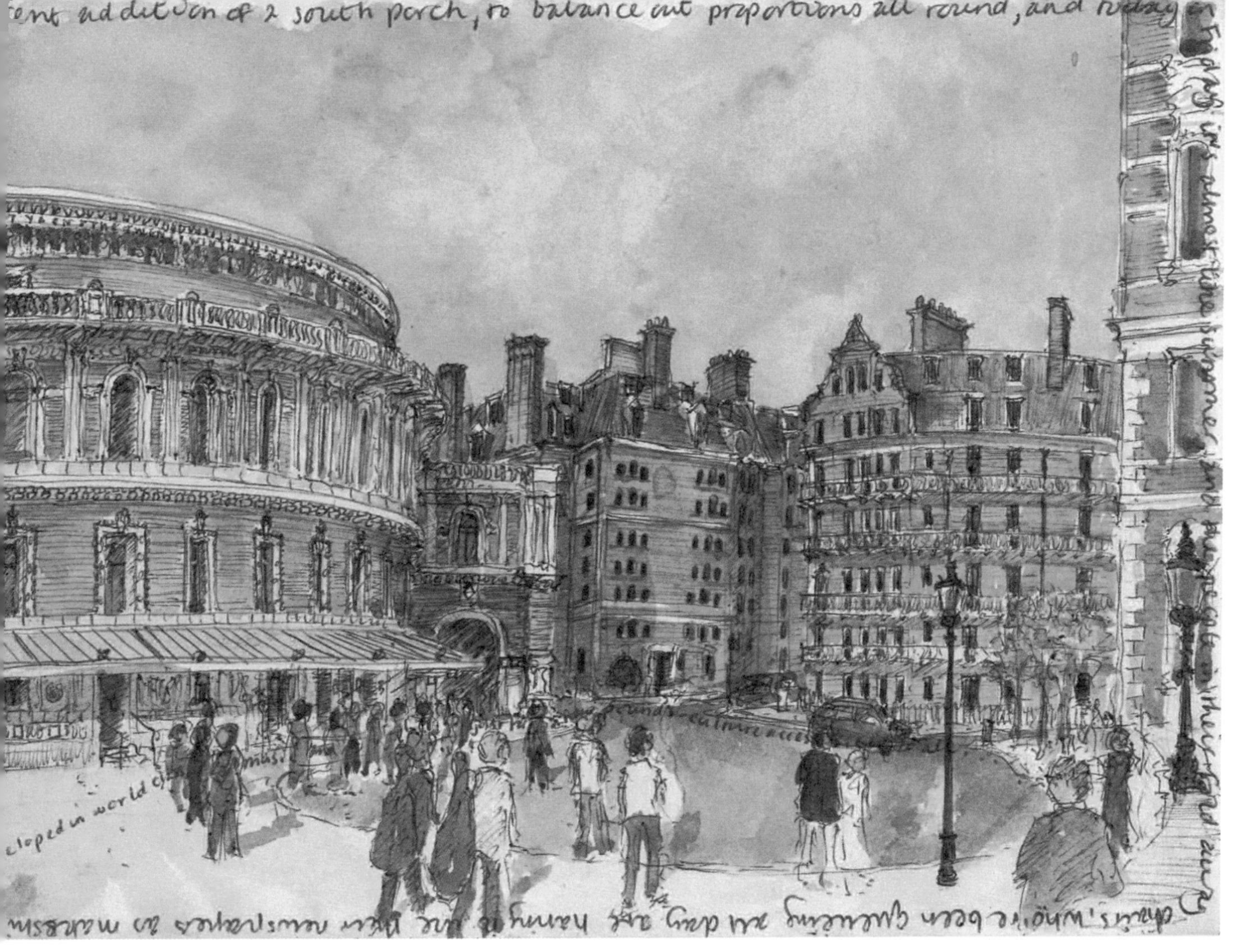
ent addition of a south porch, to balance out proportions all round, and today on

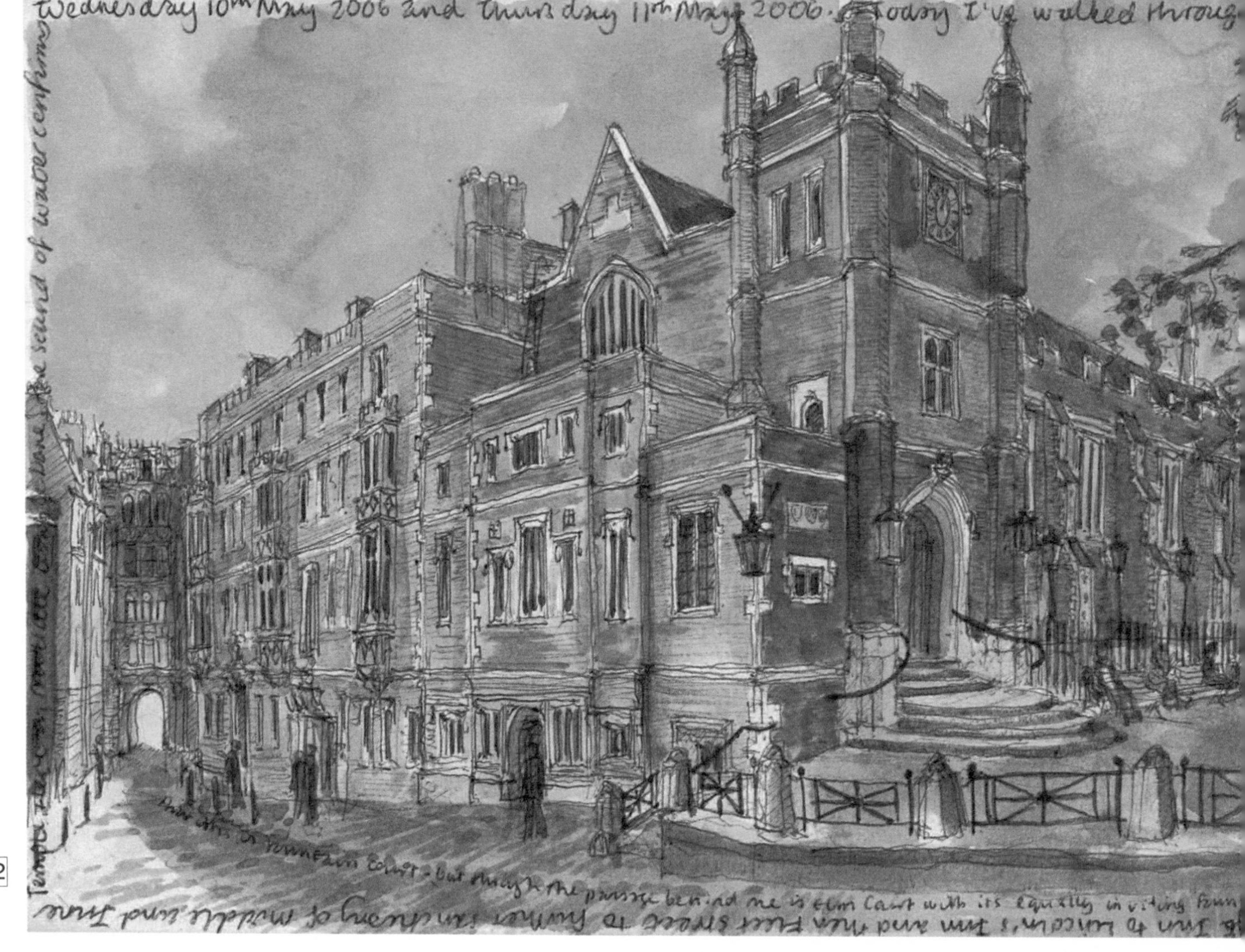
Wednesday 10th May 2006 and Thursday 11th May 2006. Today I've walked throug

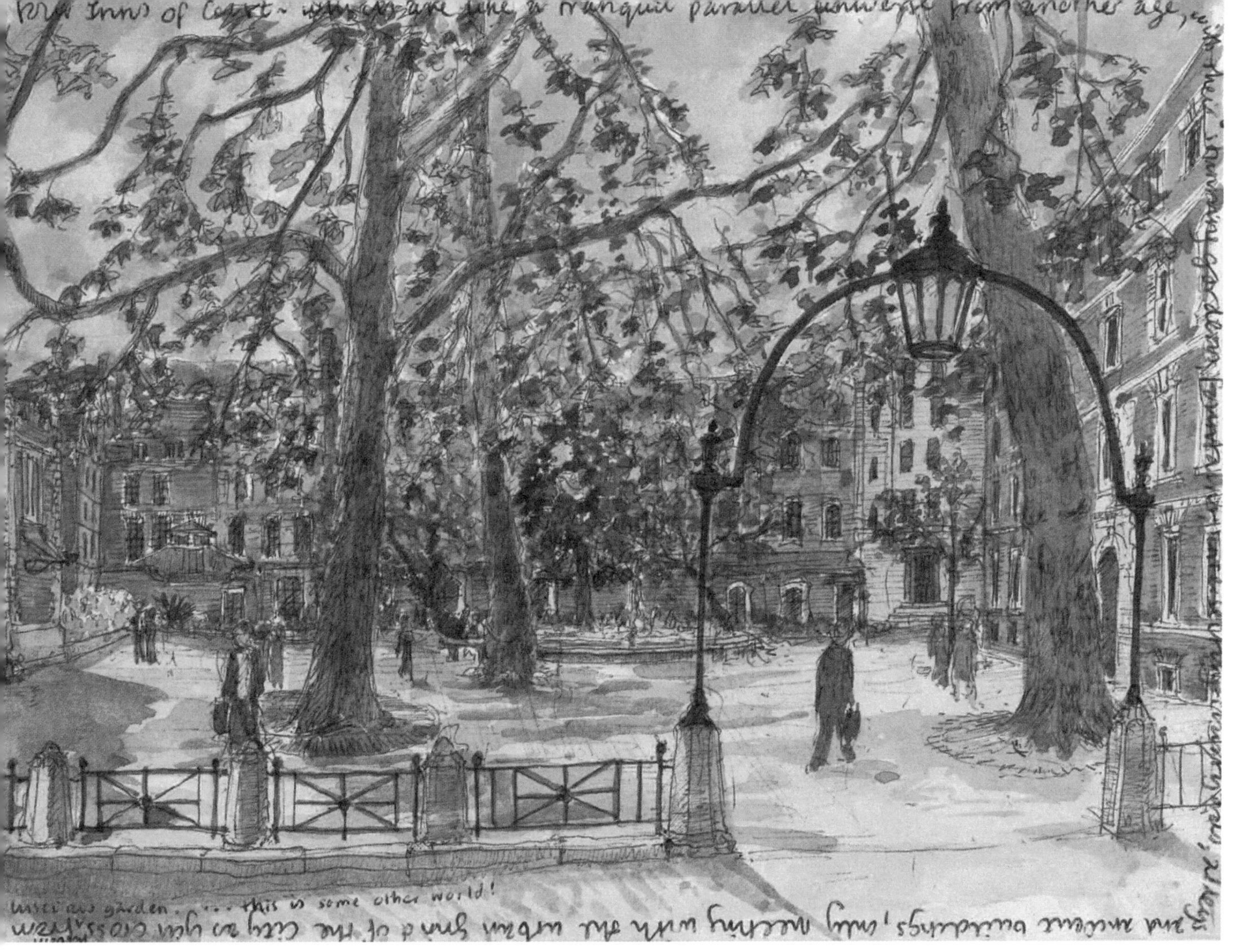

Inns of Court
like a tranquil parallel universe from another age,
garden . . . . this is some other world!

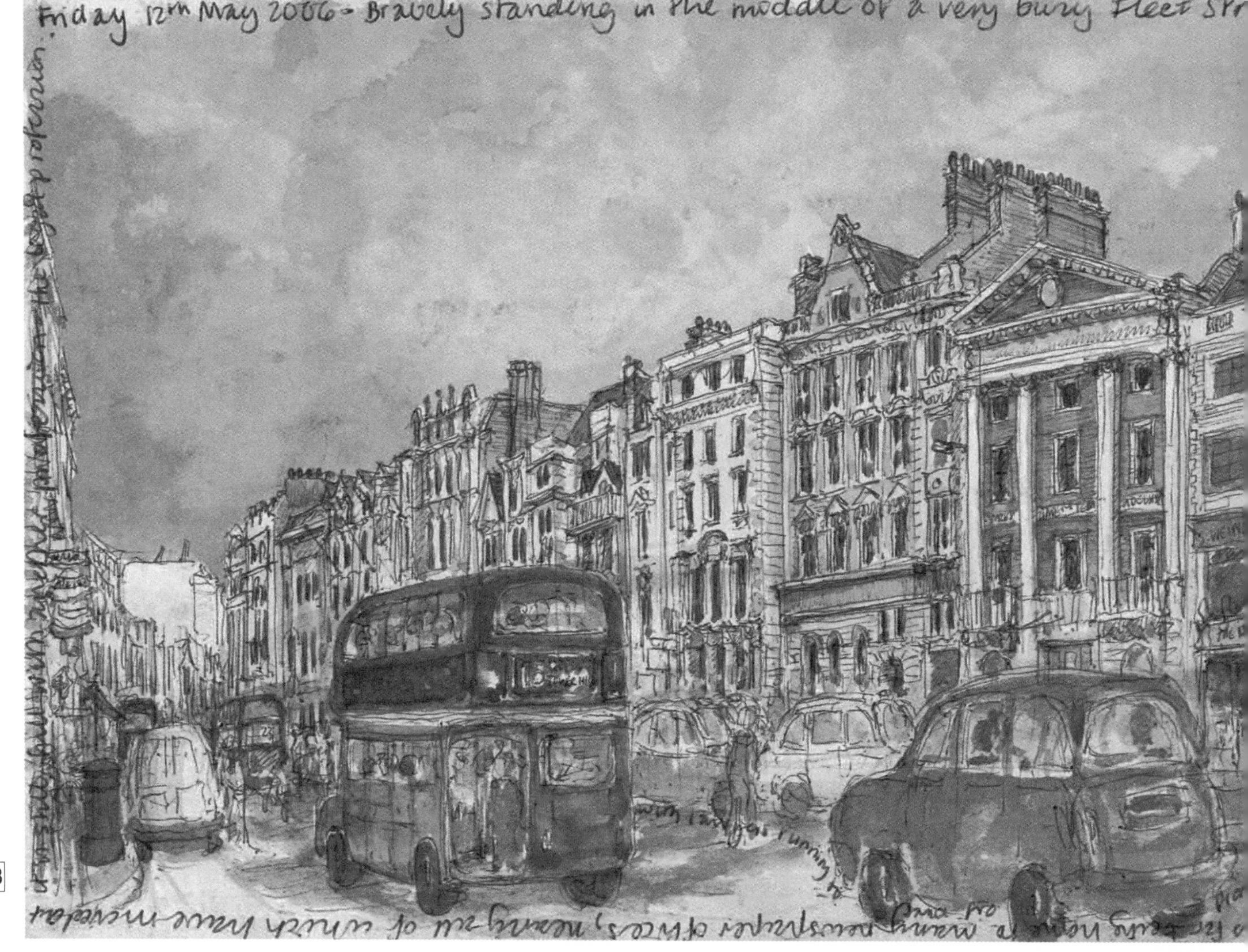
Friday 12th May 2006 - Bravely standing in the middle of a very busy Fleet Str

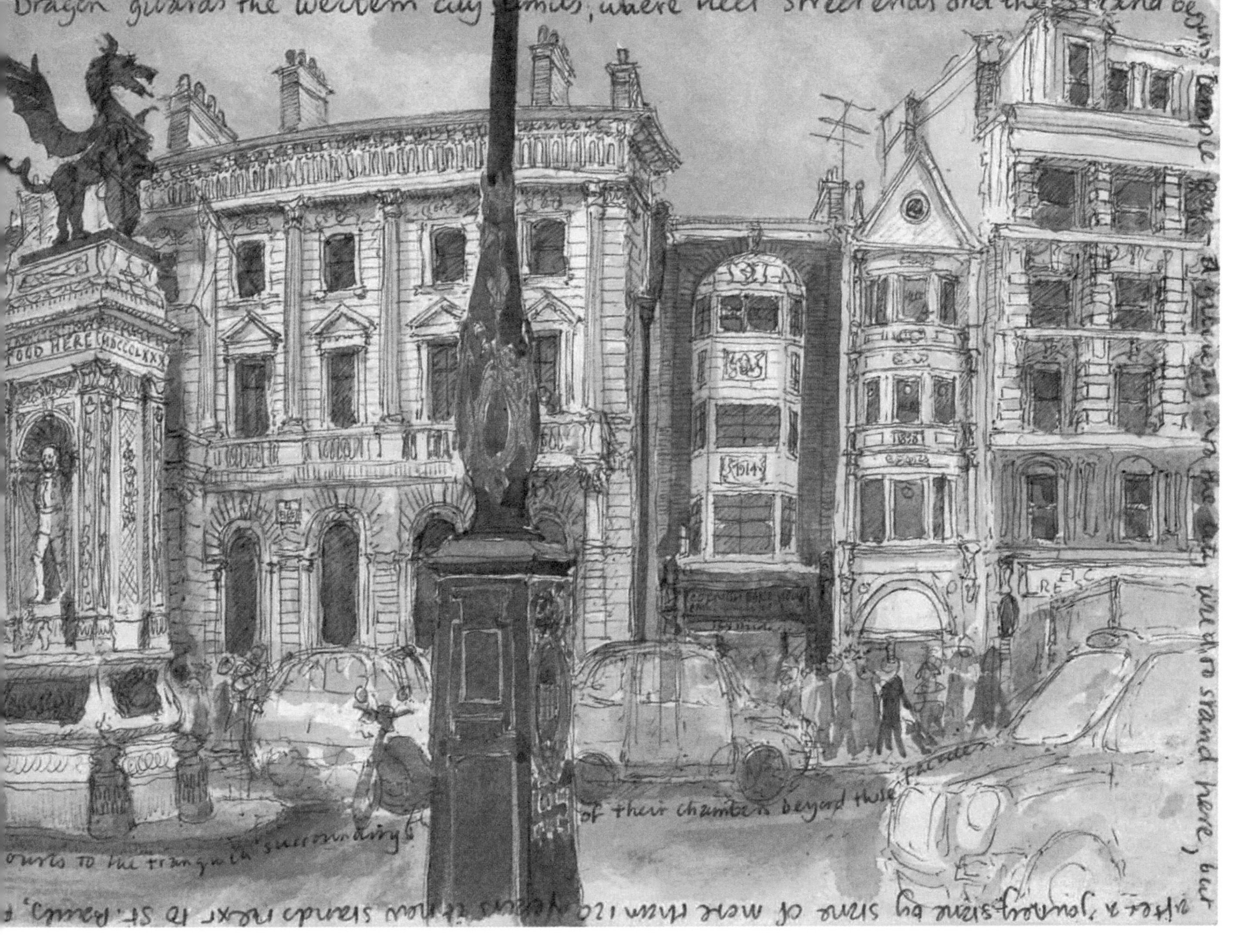

Dragon guards the western city limits, where Fleet Street ends and the Strand begins
STOOD HERE MDCCCLXXX
1914
1888
of their chambers beyond these

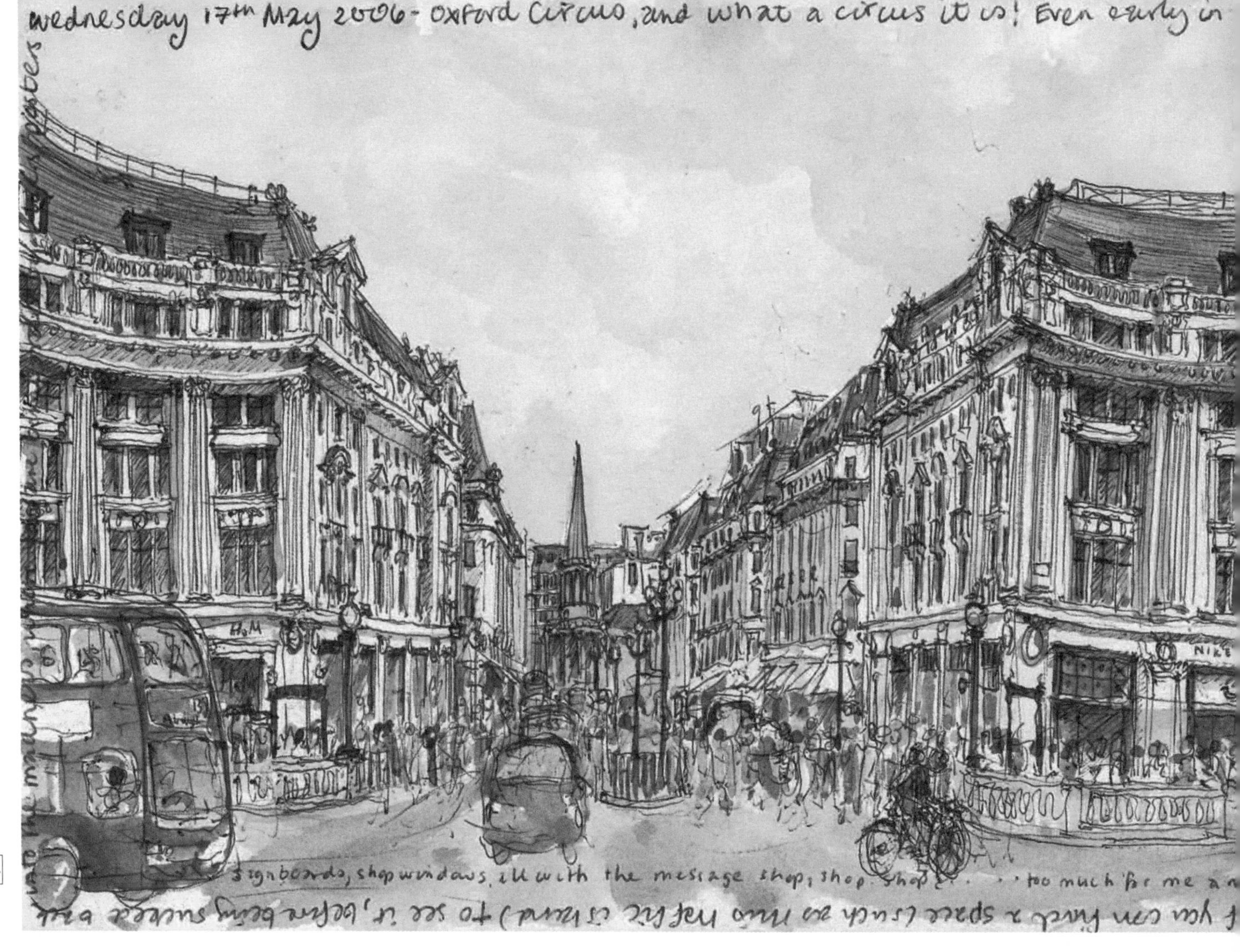

Wednesday 17th May 2006 - Oxford Circus, and what a circus it is! Even early in
H&M
NIKE
signboards, shop windows, all with the message shop, shop, shop ... too much for me

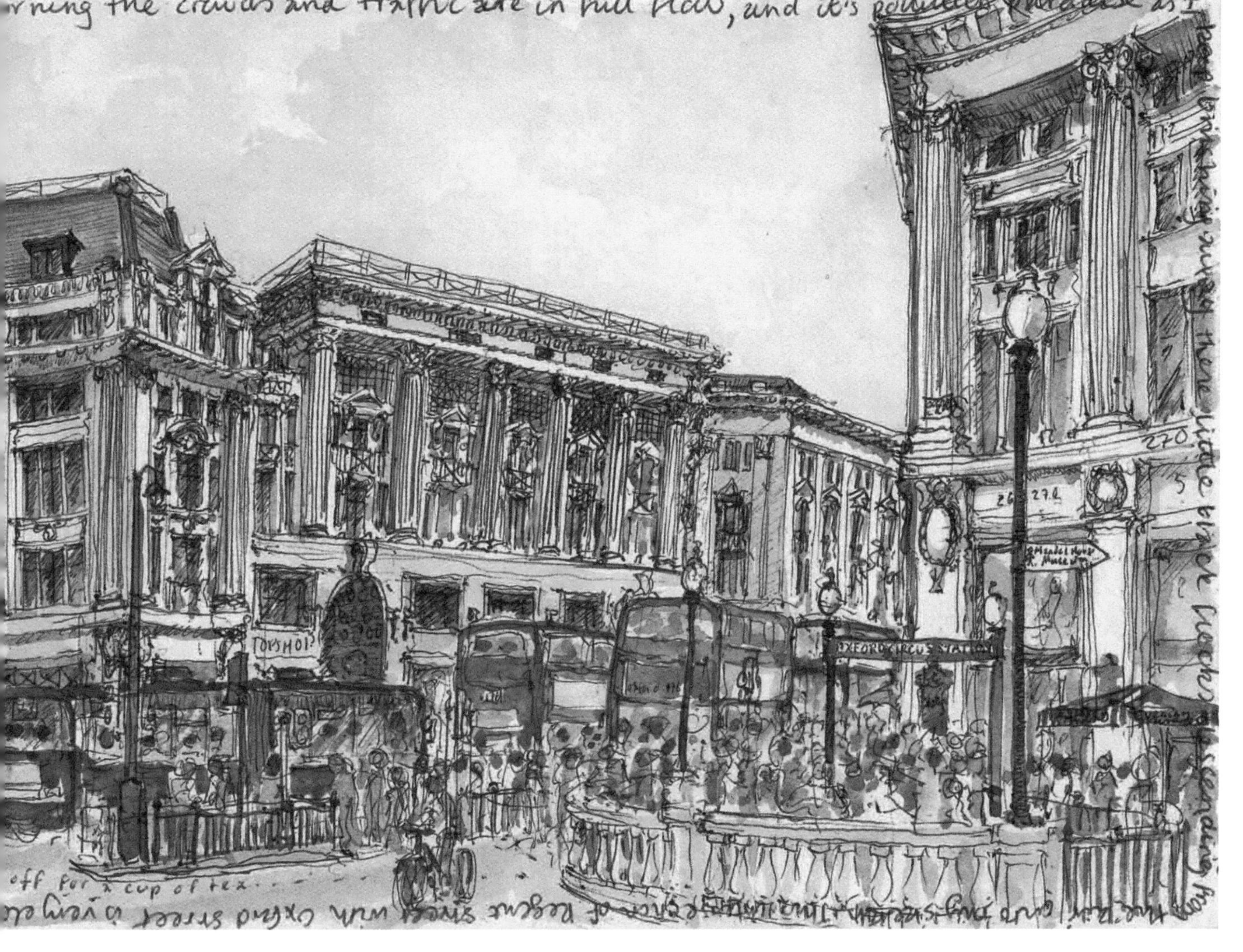
rning the crowds and traffic are in full flow, and it's pollution paradise as I
TOPSHOP
OXFORD CIRCUS STATION
270
off for a cup of tea.

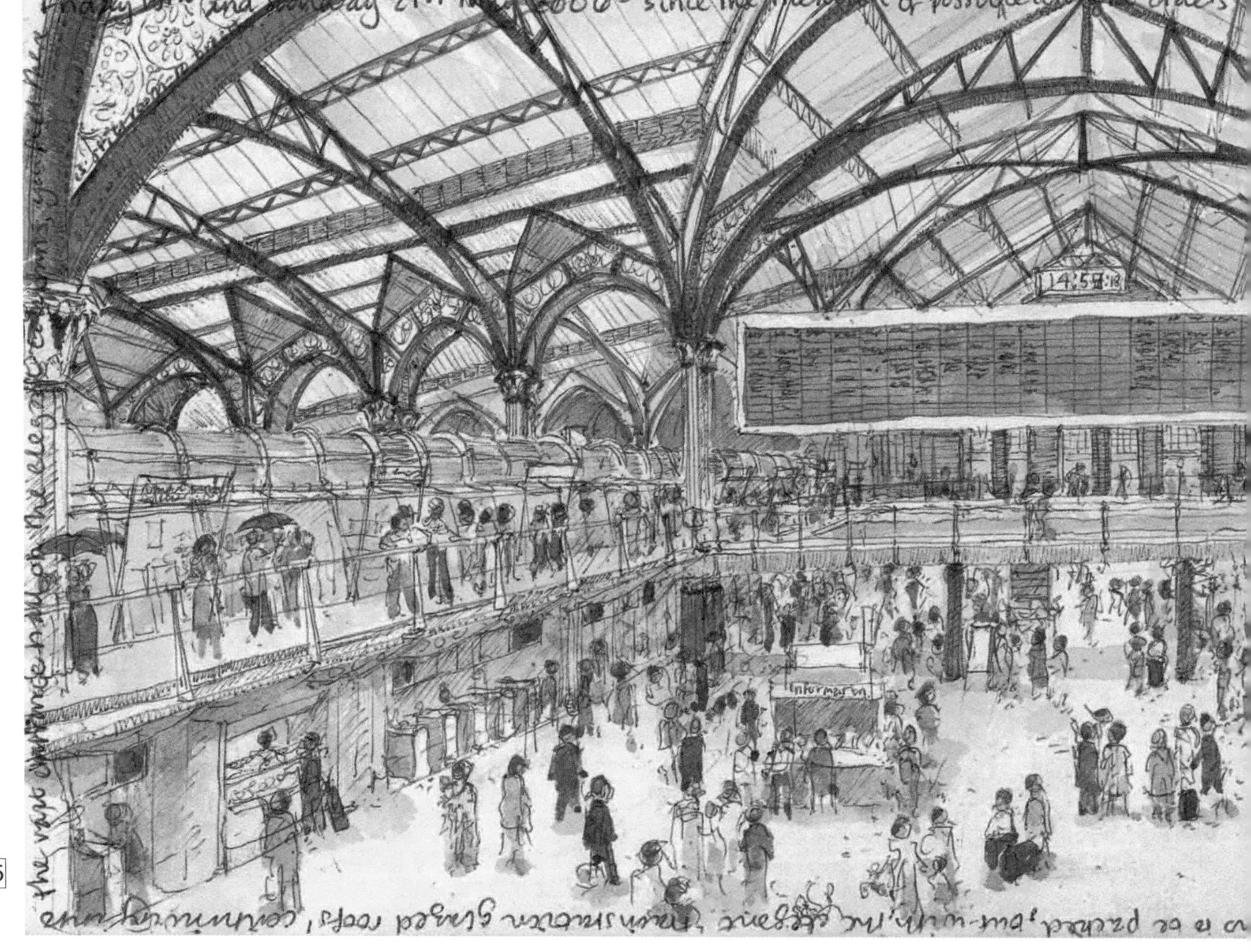

35

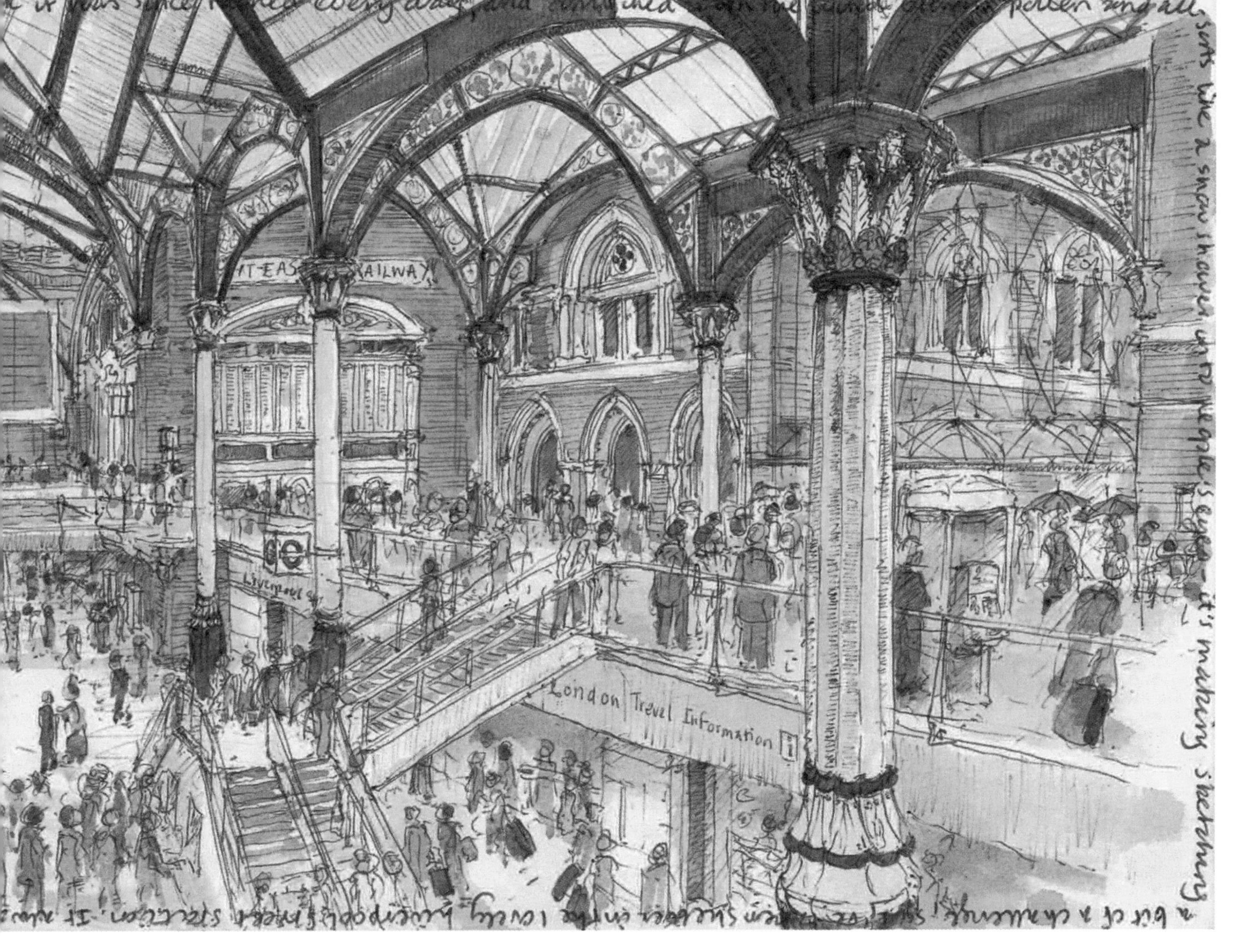
London Travel Information

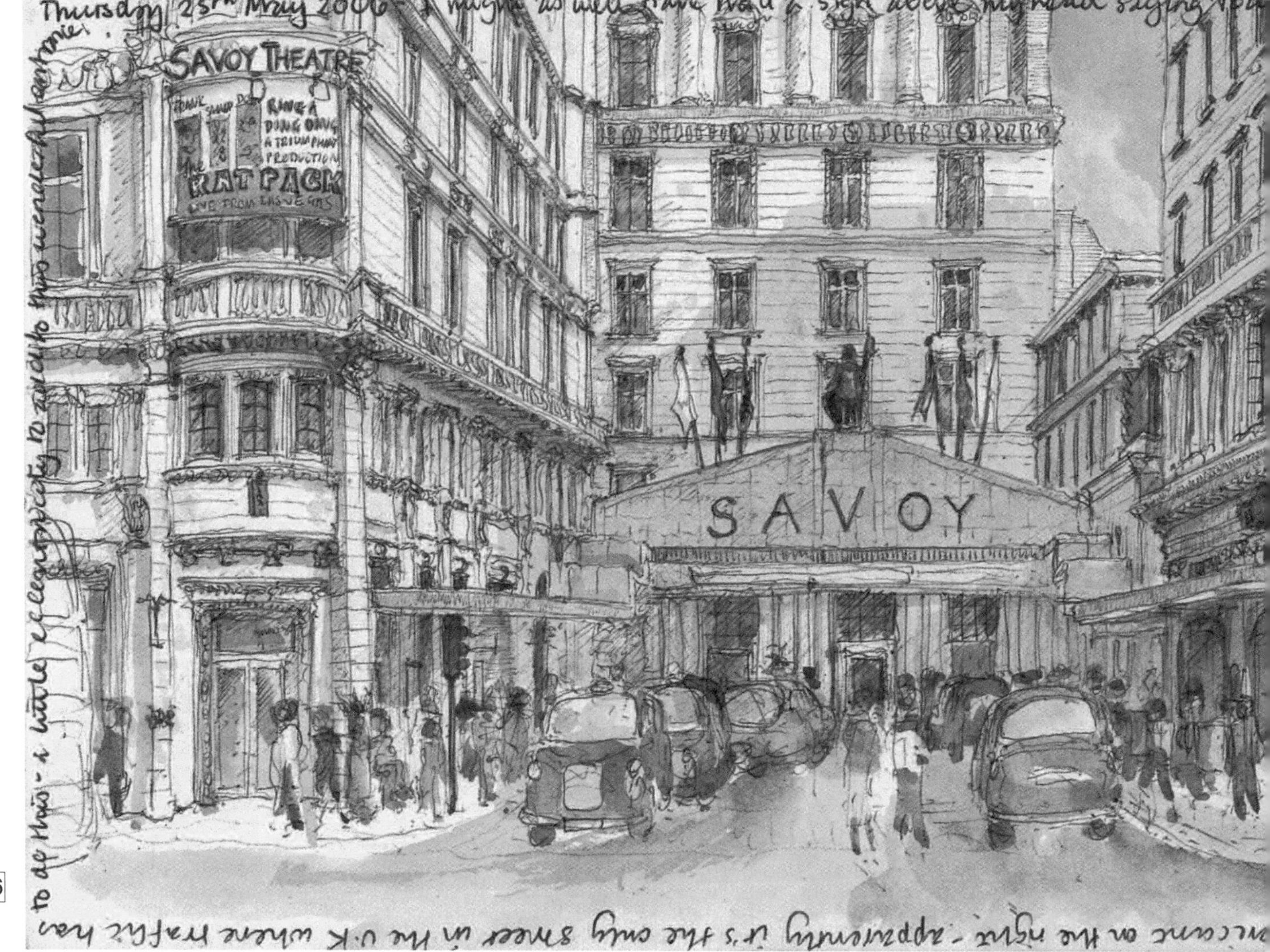
Thursday 25th May 2006 - I might as well have had a sign above my head saying
SAVOY THEATRE
RING A DING DING
A TRIUMPHANT PRODUCTION
the RAT PACK
LIVE FROM LAS VEGAS
SAVOY

36

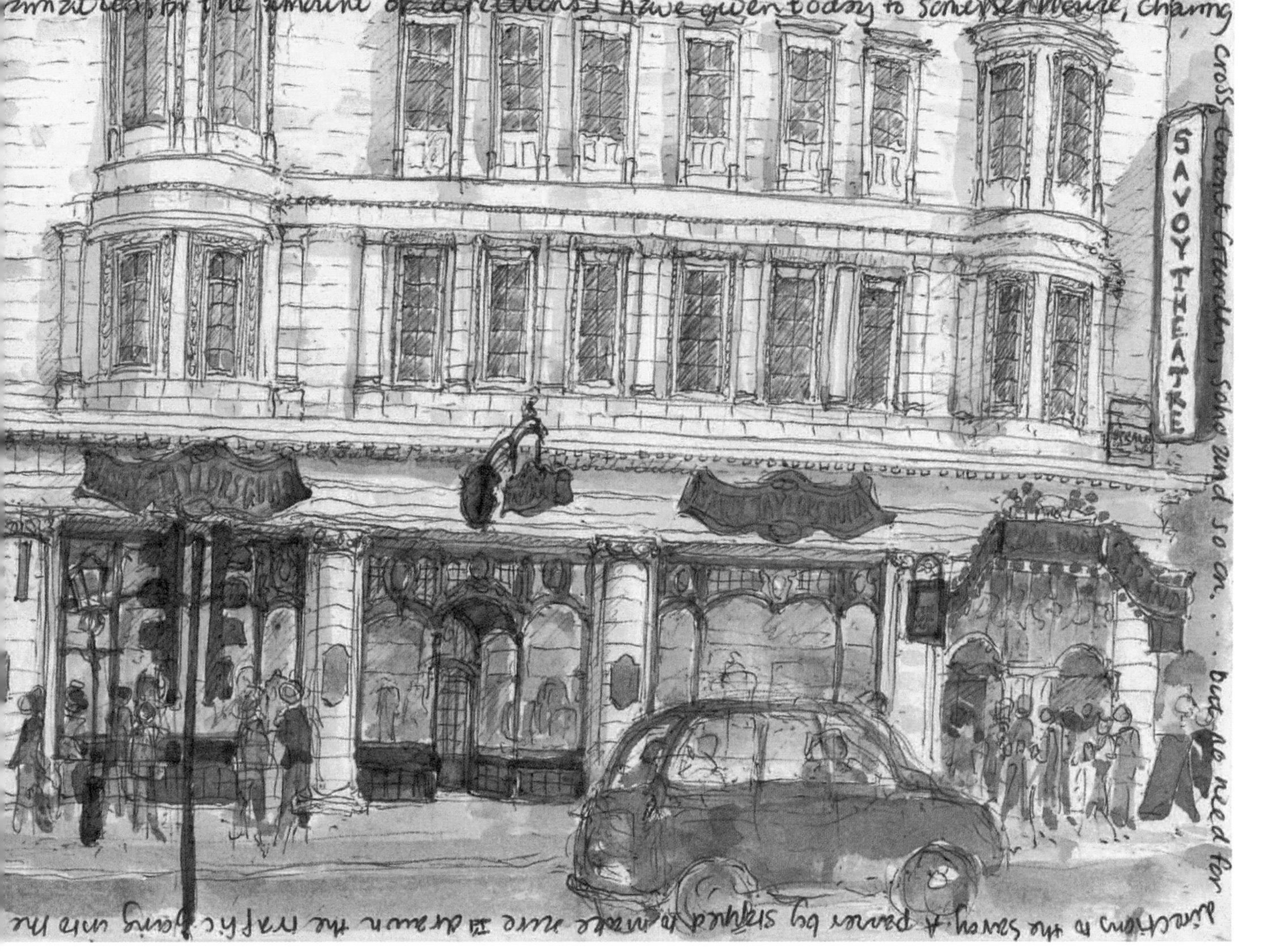
for the amount of directions I have given today to Somerset House, Charing
cross, Covent Garden, Soho and so on. . . but no need for
directions to the Savoy. A passer by stopped to make sure I drawn the traffic going into the
SAVOY THEATRE

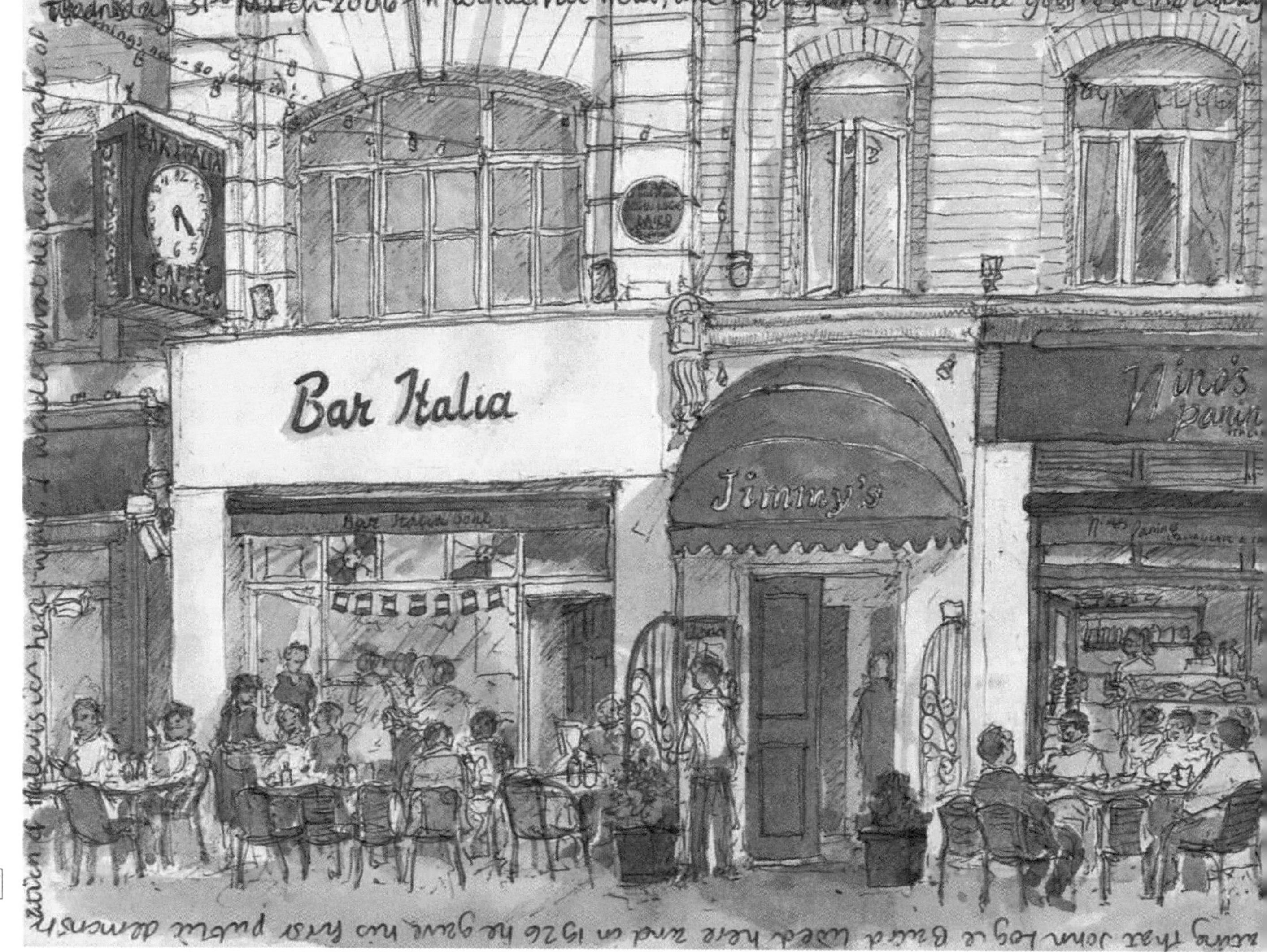

37

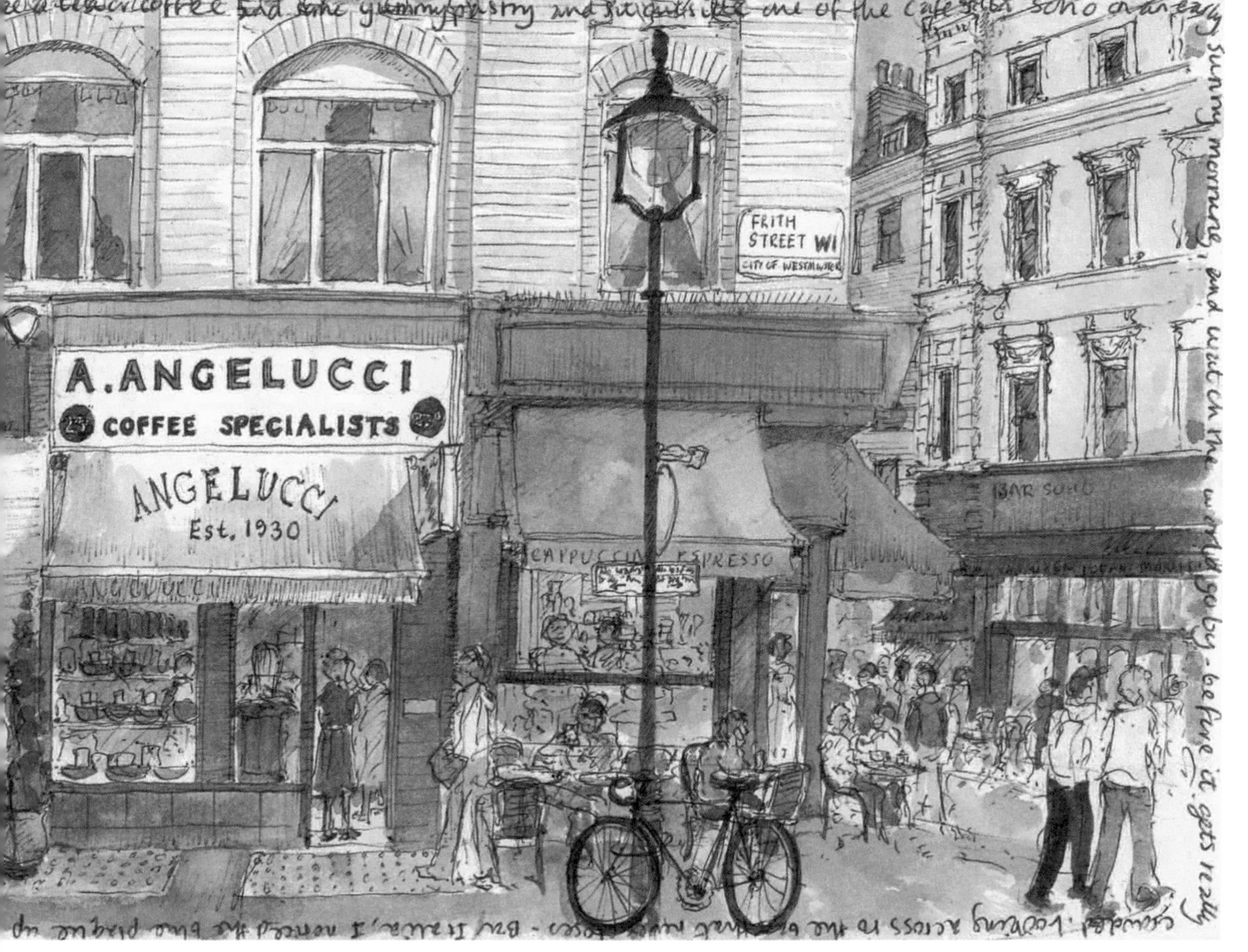
A. ANGELUCCI
COFFEE SPECIALISTS
ANGELUCCI
Est. 1930
FRITH
STREET W1
CITY OF WESTMINSTER
ESPRESSO
BAR SOHO
sunny morning, and watch the world go by - before it gets really

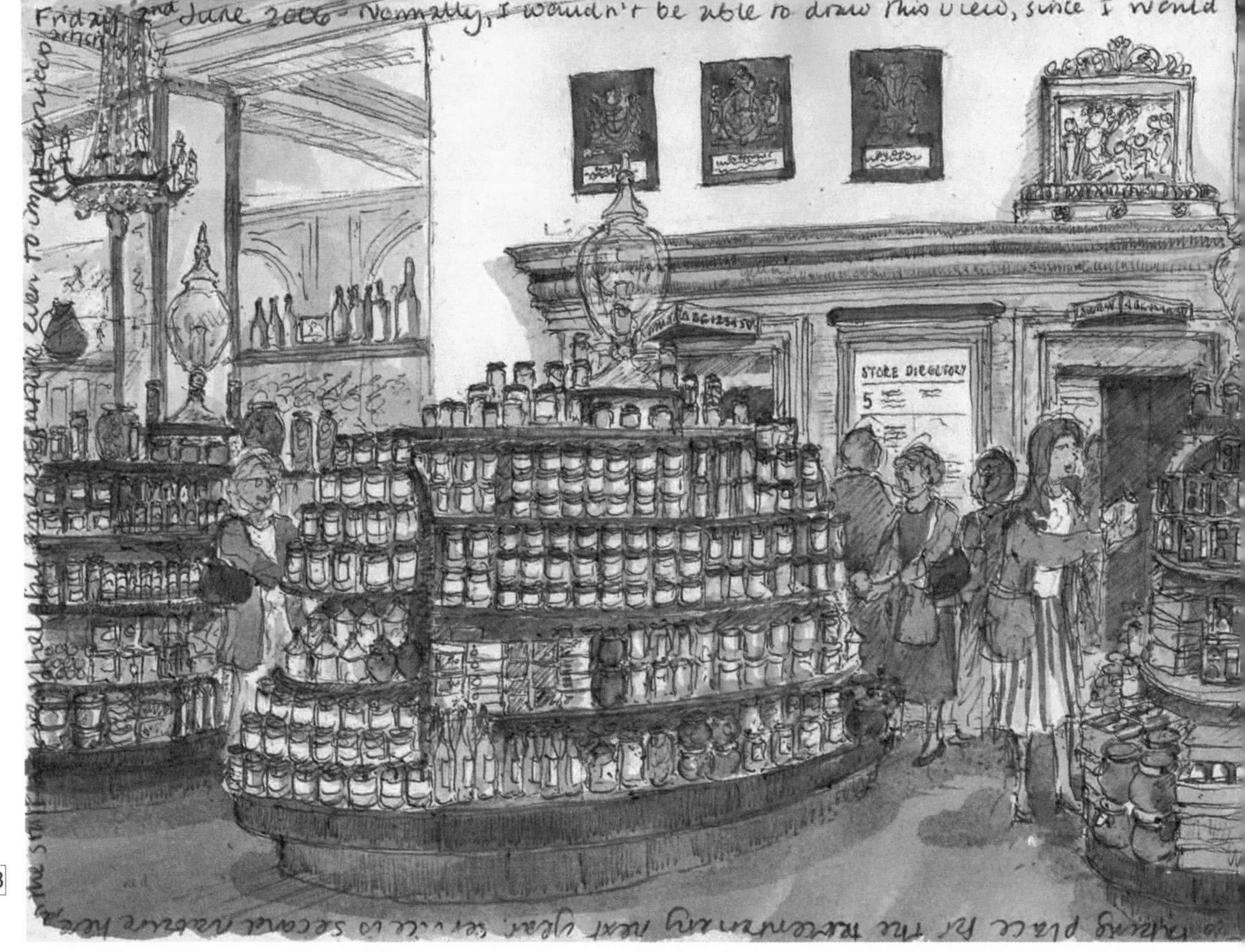
Friday 2nd June 2006 - Normally, I wouldn't be able to draw this view, since I would
STORE DIRECTORY
5

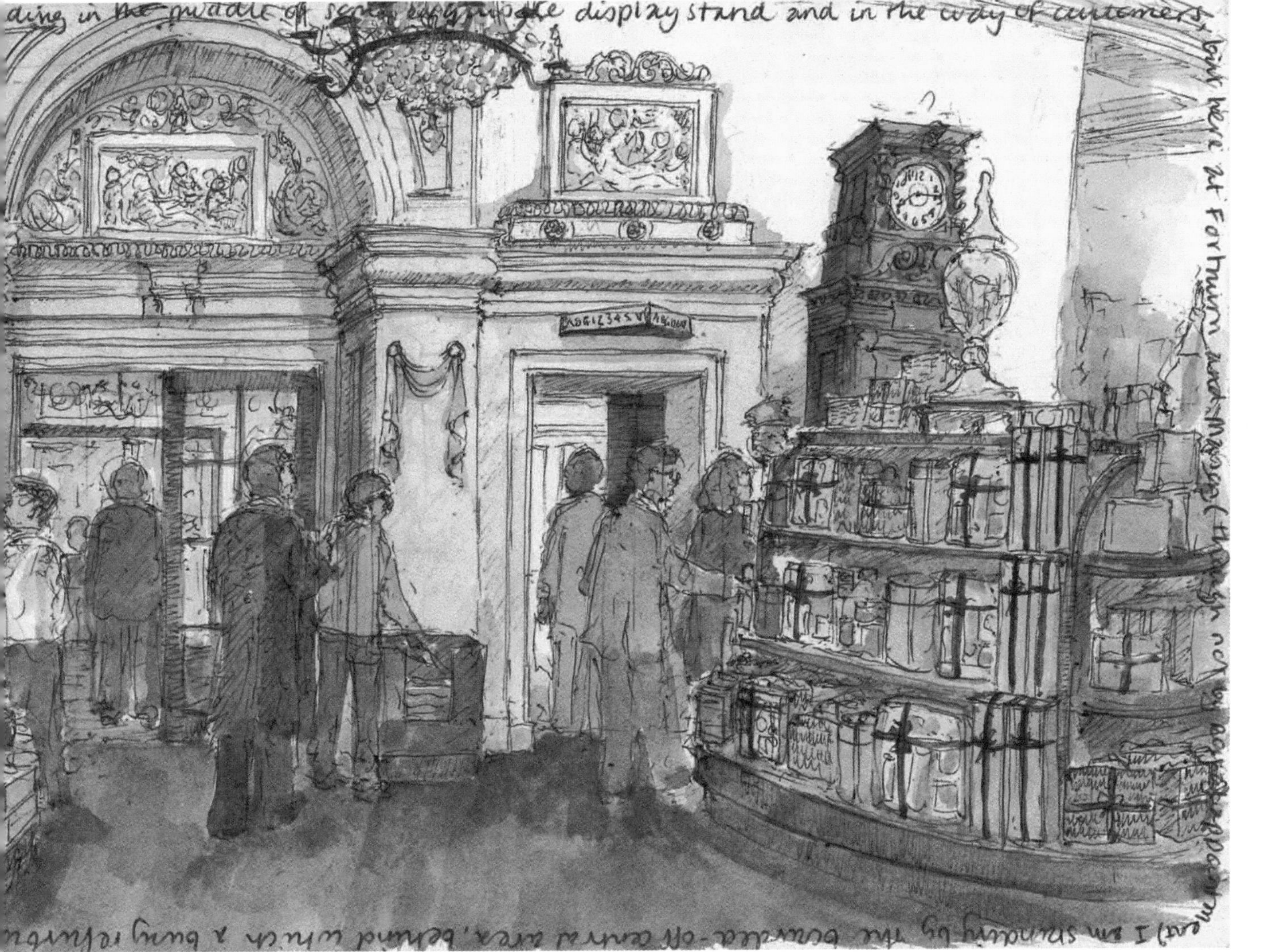
display stand and in the
at Fortnum and Mason
I am standing by the

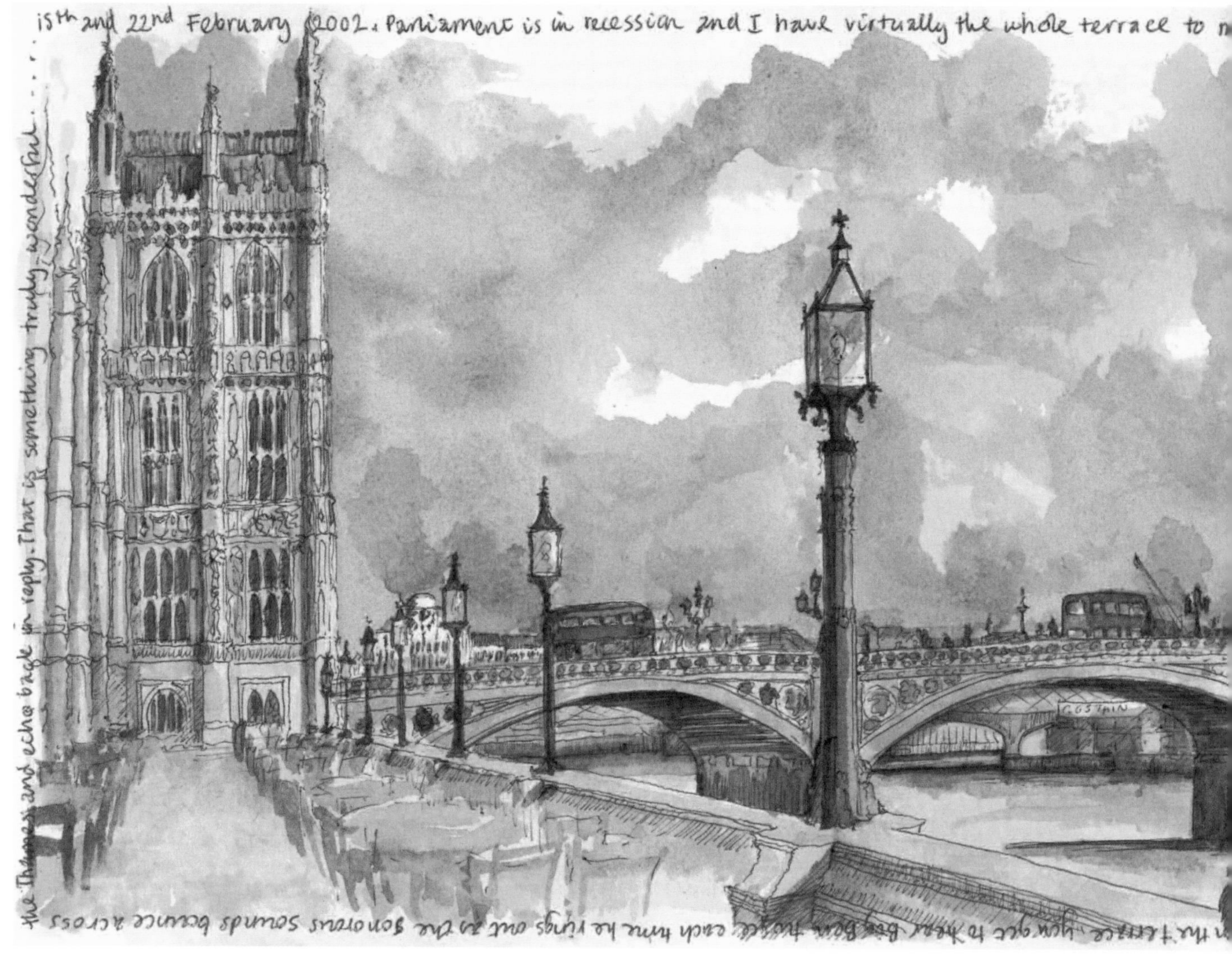
15th and 22nd February 2002. Parliament is in recession and I have virtually the whole terrace to
the terrace you get to hear Big Ben twice each time he rings out as the sonorous sounds bounce across
the Thames and echo back in reply. That is something truly wonderful . . .
COSTAIN

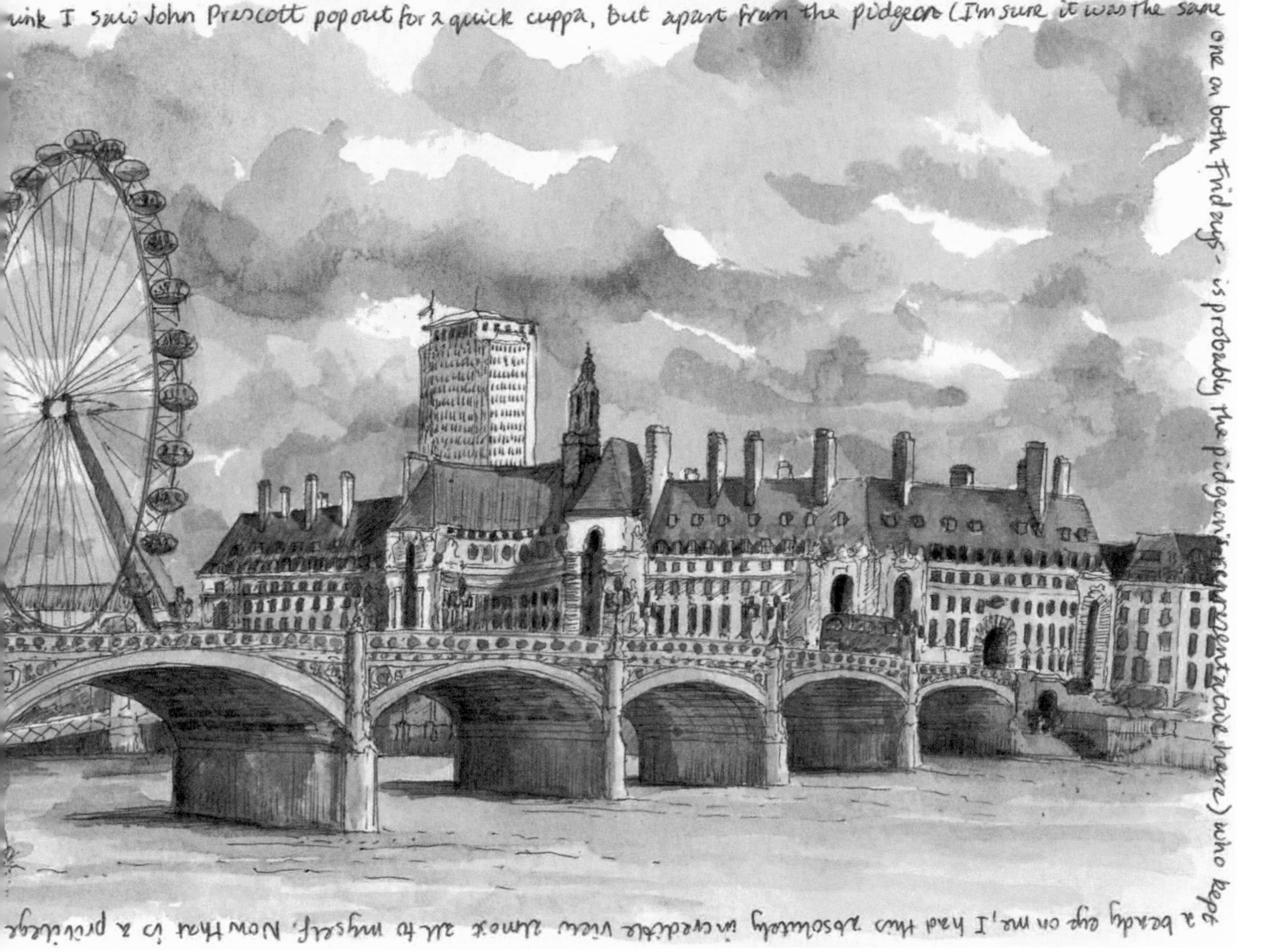
ink I saw John Prescott pop out for a quick cuppa, but apart from the pidgeon (I'm sure it was the same
one on both Fridays - is probably the pidgeon's representative here) who kept
a beady eye on me, I had this absolutely incredible view almost all to myself. Now that is a privilege

Friday June 21st 2002 So today our World Cup dreams are dashed for another four years and there is

summer spirit about and I hope this remains well life goes on and I was amazed sitting here

by Westminster Bridge to see a cormorant in the fast flowing river

diving for two sizeable fish which he had trouble devouring as they writhed about. Poor things.

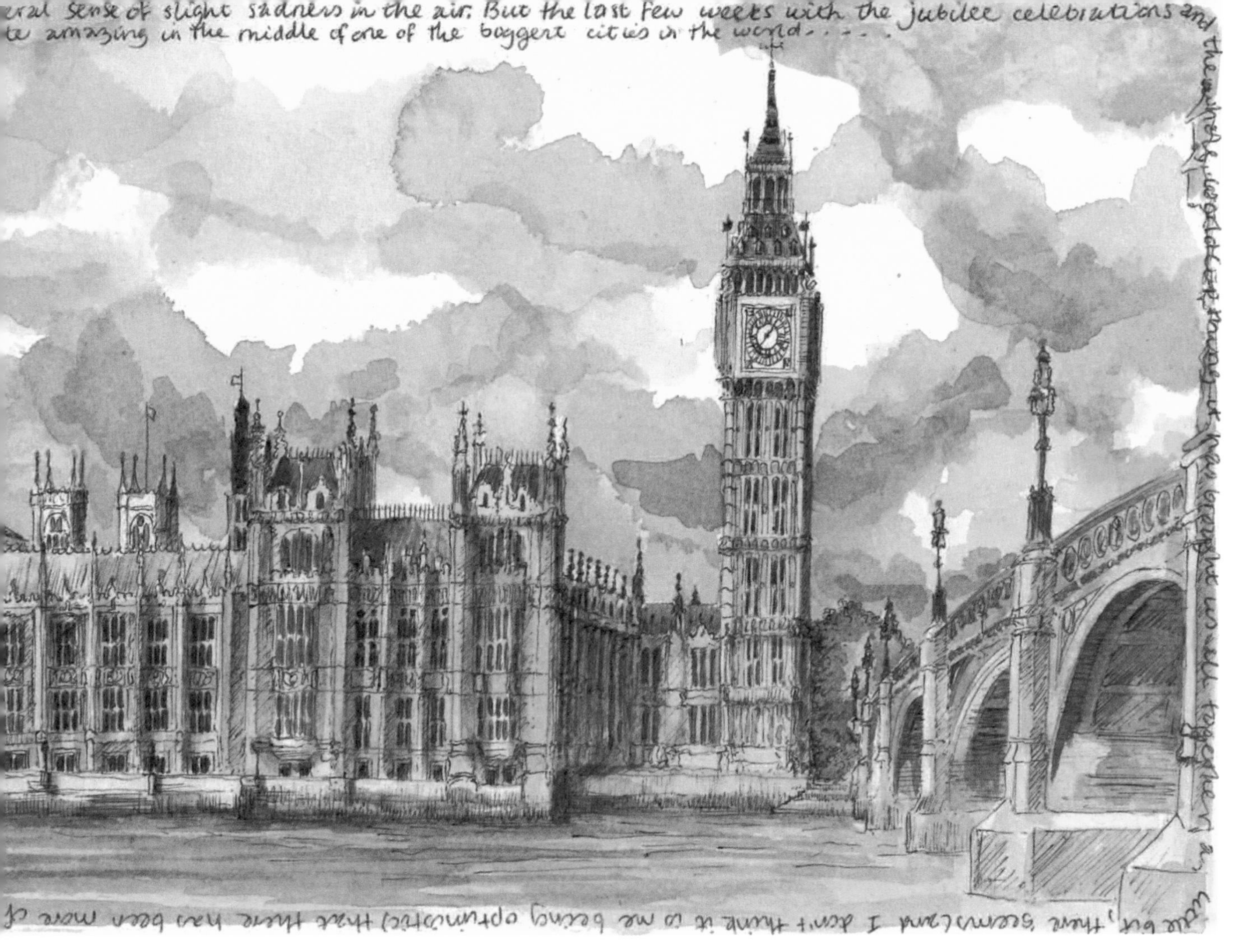
eral sense of slight sadness in the air. But the last few weeks with the jubilee celebrations and
te amazing in the middle of one of the biggest cities in the world....

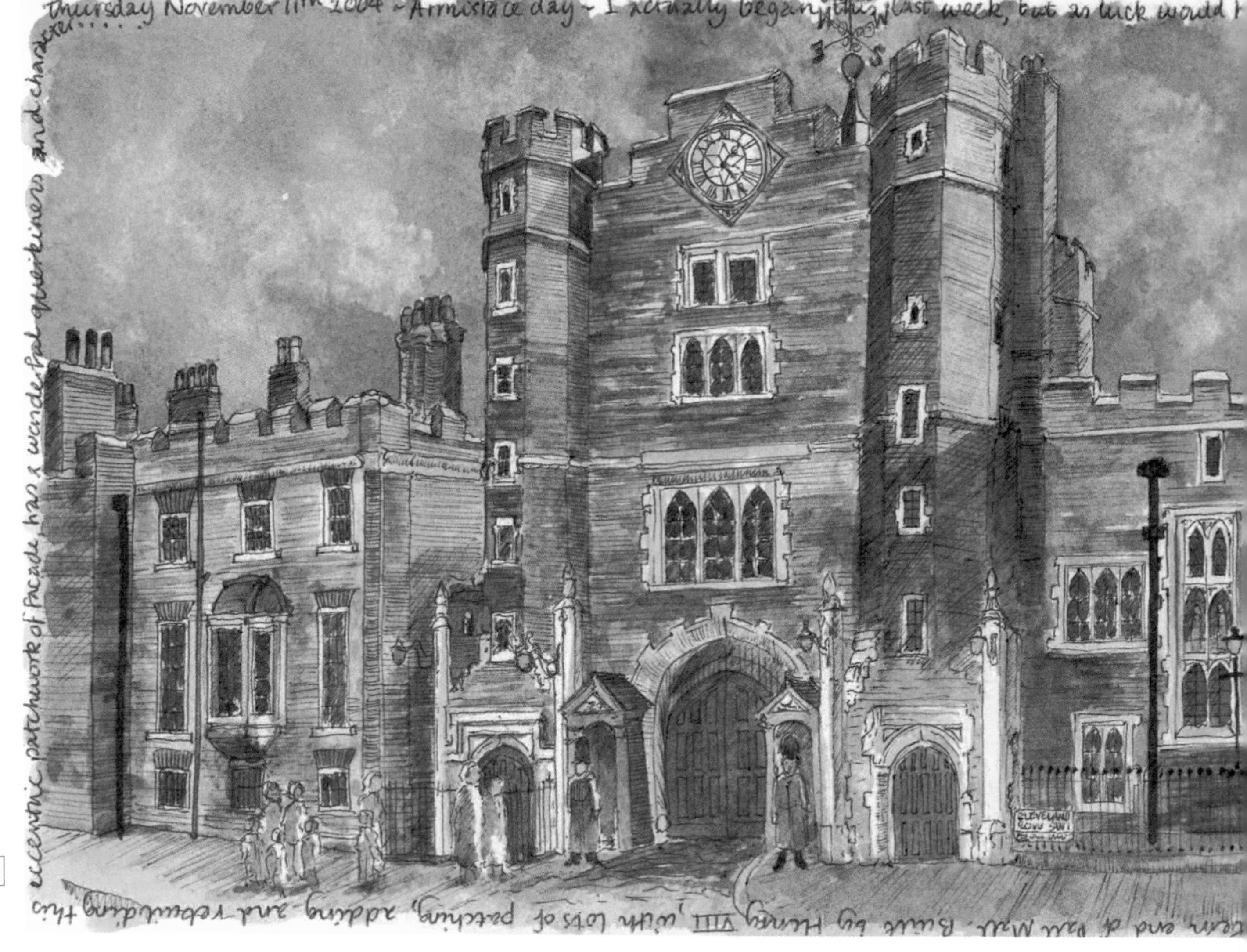
Thursday November 11th 2004 ~ Armistice day ~ I actually began this last week, but as luck would
end of Pall Mall. Built by Henry VIII, with lots of patching, adding and rebuilding this
eccentric patchwork of facade, has a wonderful quirkiness and character....
CLEVELAND ROW SW1

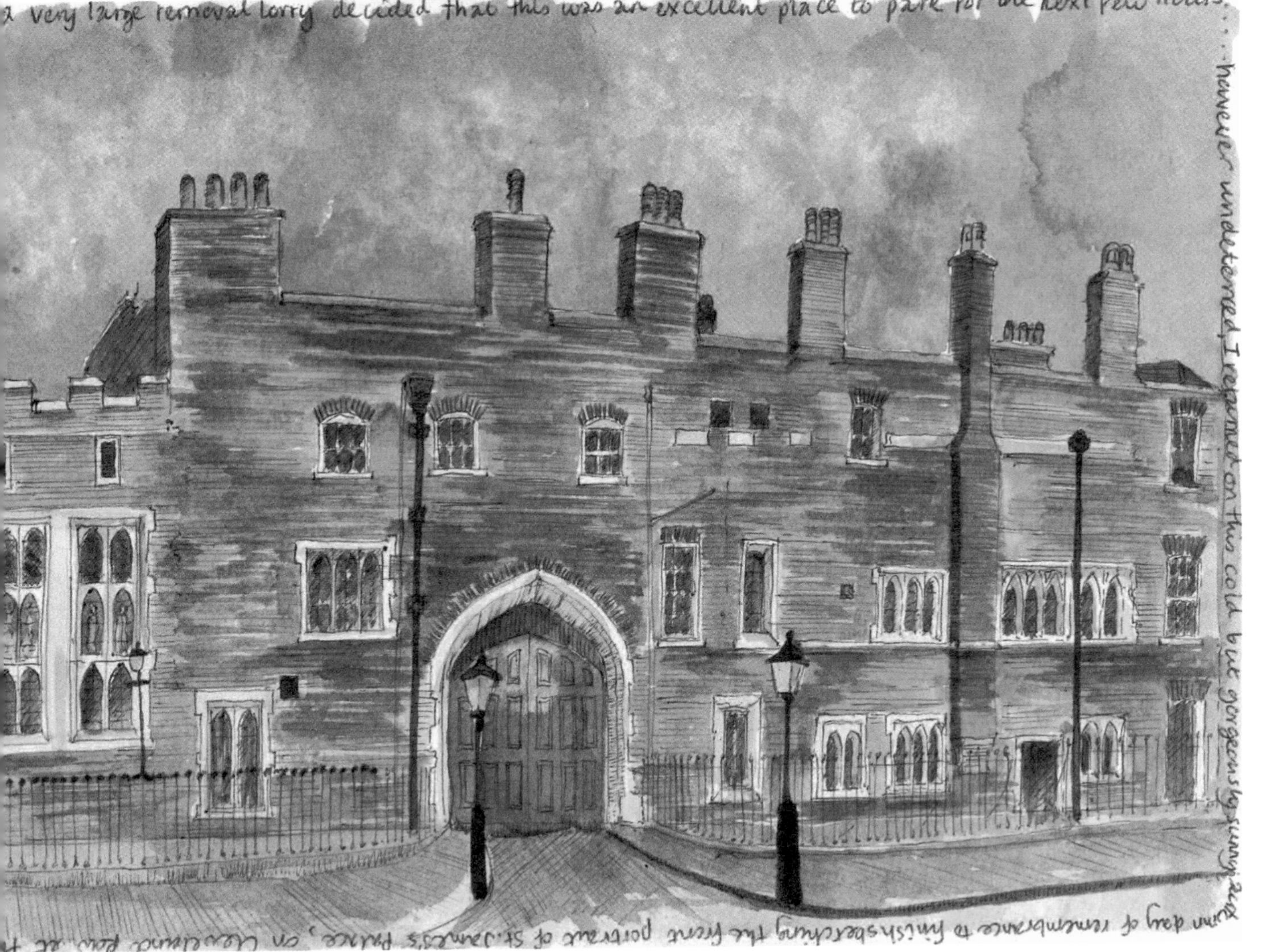
a very large removal lorry decided that this was an excellent place to park for the next few hours...
...however undeterred, I returned on this cold but gorgeously sunny autumn day of remembrance to finish sketching the front portrait of St. James's Palace, on Cleveland Row, at t

INTRODUCTION

I am a London based artist and architect. My passion is sketching and painting the world around me.

My art teacher's advice, 'always keep a sketchbook on you', has remained with me and I now have a collection of them, all drawn with an ordinary black biro and painted with my small field box of watercolours, not much larger than a mobile telephone.

London in Landscape has been a labour of love. Over the last year or so I've been out in all weathers to capture a few of the many diverse and wonderful scenes in our amazing city – in snowy Ludgate Hill, at the top of a windy Monument, amid the bustle of Fleet Street, in manic Oxford Circus, in the packed stands of the old Arsenal Stadium… I sketch in my book as much as I can of what is going on around me. Sometimes I paint on site too but otherwise I complete my work at home relying on my memory of several hours spent in each place. My notes around the edges are observations made while sketching.

London in Landscape is a collection of forty-two sketches which I began in 2001. In that year I was awarded a Winston Churchill Memorial Trust Fellowship which gave me the chance to make an artist's journey to World Heritage cities and other sites. I set out from France eastwards through Europe, Iran, Uzbekistan, India and Nepal, recording my journey in the pages of my sketchbook diary. I continued the World Heritage theme with a venture to Havana in Cuba, and closer to home a community project along Hadrian's Wall, again recording everything in my sketch-books. On my return to London, I was privileged to sketch in and around the Palace of Westminster in 2002 and 2003. In 2004 I was appointed artist in residence at the Athenaeum Club and in 2005 I was selected as the 'Young Cricket Artist' by Marylebone Cricket Club and granted the 'freedom' of Lord's Ground for a year.

In the metropolis of London, constantly on the move, all bustle and noise, it has been a real joy to be lost in the 'spirit of place' for hour after hour and simply to sketch. I hope readers will enjoy this book as much as I have enjoyed creating it and perhaps some will visit the scenes I have sketched and hopefully discover something new…

1. St Paul's from Ludgate Hill

MONDAY 28TH FEBRUARY AND TUESDAY 1ST MARCH 2005

Accompanied by flurries of snow, I've taken the lovely walk from Angel down to St Paul's, shivering in the winter skies. I still find it amazing that while Mr Wren was presiding over the rather monumental task of St Paul's, he was also sorting out dozens of other churches, such as St-Martin-within-Ludgate, who's nestled himself in halfway up the hill.

2. Inside Leadenhall Market

WEDNESDAY 2ND AND THURSDAY 3RD MARCH 2005

Even though the delightful dragons on their perches look a bit miffed that the icy gales have taken their fiery breath away, life still goes on below. Smart suits swish by and – incredibly, as I stand here freezing in my layers – the click, click on the cobbles of sharp stiletto heels.

3. Lime Street Passage

THURSDAY 3RD MARCH AND MONDAY 7TH MARCH 2005

Sweeping oh-so-gracefully into Leadenhall Market, it's such a haven on a very human scale from the towering and imposing city that surrounds it. The vibrant colours are a beacon and a welcome warmer to the pale winter colours around.

4. Camden Passage

SATURDAY 5TH MARCH 2005

Camden Passage comes alive every Wednesday, Saturday and Sundays, when all the shops' treasures spill onto the passageway and mingle with the bric-à-brac stalls and the people of many nationalities browsing through the wares, which are as diverse as they are.

5. Borough Market

THURSDAY 10TH AND FRIDAY 11TH MARCH 2005

The last time I sketched here was, I think, in 1992, and I remember signing a petition to save the then very dilapidated Borough Market from being devoured by expanding train tracks, which pick their way through and around the market at high level. What a difference now – yesterday, not a market day, it was quiet and you could linger over the complete mish-mash of columns and complex roofs; but today, you are swept away by the crowds packing the space between the fabulous food stalls.

6. View from the Tate Gallery

WEDNESDAY 9TH MARCH 2005

Members of the Tate Gallery are very lucky to have this view all to themselves. I'm very lucky because I have friends who are members, and the Tate very generously allows them to bring a guest – lucky me! Get here early and the view is just for you and your cup of tea.

7. Columbia Road

SUNDAY 13TH MARCH 2005

The fabulous Columbia Road Flower Market. You know you are getting near as you see plants of all shapes and sizes, and bunches of colourful flowers pass by in the opposite direction, precariously carried by their human purchasers buried underneath.

8. Number 38 Routemasters outside Victoria Station

TUESDAY SEPTEMBER 27TH 2005

I've been meaning to draw these beautiful Routemaster beasties for ages, but the relentless pursuit of technology and ever-demanding health and safety legislation has finally compelled me into action: in a few weeks' time this symbol of London, famous the world over, rolls into retirement. As I sit here sketching, each bus draws up with its rich rumble and roars off to the next round – they're not ready to stop!

9. Clapton Bus Garage

MONDAY OCTOBER 2ND 2005

This is where the buses come to rest, recuperate, be revived and restored, so they can rev and roar off into the relentless traffic. By the end of the month this scene will be no more and they'll all be looking for new homes. It's all very sad.

10. Piccadilly Circus

MONDAY 14TH AND TUESDAY 15TH NOVEMBER 2005

Piccadilly Circus is always so lively in all its elegant and garish glory. Mr Nash's refined Regent Street sweeps gracefully round to crash into the electric-city in its full Technicolor glory. Eros, obviously fazed by the pixelated Coca-Cola bottles, chooses to shoot his arrows in the opposite direction.

11. Burlington Arcade

WEDNESDAY 14TH DECEMBER 2005

This splendid arcade, with its smart elegant and pristine shop fronts is watched over by the Beadles with their top hats who ensure that a genteel air of calm and order is maintained against the furious frenzy out on Piccadilly.

12. Trafalgar Square

TUESDAY 29TH DECEMBER AND MONDAY 9TH JANUARY 2006

Over Christmas I bought Trafalgar Square for the bargain price of £280 or thereabouts, and did very well from it. Regrettably this was only on the Monopoly board – oh, if only…

13. Smithfield Market

TUESDAY 24TH JANUARY 2006

It's certainly a much smarter and more civilised joint (ha-ha) today than in its more gruesome past as a place of public executions, animal slaughters and so on. Though it's still the meat market, it's now surrounded by a buzz of creative industries and trendy bars and cafés.

14. Buckingham Palace

THURSDAY 19TH, FRIDAY 20TH AND SATURDAY 21ST JANUARY 2006

What a difference a day with a little sunshine can make to the seemingly eternal grey, damp, drizzly January. On Thursday, rain stopped play. On Friday, the sun was out, the guards were out (Changing of the Guard); even the unicorns and lions guarding the gates to the Queen's London home seemed to be smiling, as they performed their duties to keep the continuous crowds of tourists at a polite distance.

15. St Bartholomew the Great

THURSDAY 26TH AND FRIDAY 27TH JANUARY

When it all gets too much, this is where I come to. Precious peace and heavenly harmony surround anyone who enters this lovely, lovely place.

16. Chinatown

TUESDAY 31ST JANUARY 2006

At the Heart of Chinatown, beautifully bedecked in luminous lanterns and flags depicting all the different animals of the Chinese calendar. I've discovered that I'm a rooster, but am hoping I won't be joining the other roasted fowl in the restaurant windows.

17. Bank

SUNDAY 5TH AND MONDAY 6TH FEBRUARY 2006

One place, but sketched on two very different days. On Sunday morning I can see the City sleep peacefully, save for the occasional passer-by asking for directions. On Monday, however, I daren't move an inch as buses, taxis and vans hurtle by and people hurry past me to the next meeting – the City is awake and pulsating!

18. View from the National Portrait Gallery

THURSDAY 9TH AND FRIDAY 10TH FEBRUARY 2006

Several years ago, common mortals could come up here to the rooftop restaurant and stand in a set-aside corner of the room and gobble up this glorious view, without having to gobble any food. Now however you have to book a table, unless like me you write to the right people and come in as the sun rises and London begins to wake up – and the restaurant staff are already preparing for another busy day.

19. The Reading Room in the British Museum

FRIDAY 3RD MARCH 2006

Now it's open to the public, you don't have to be a great intellectual reader to enjoy this fabulous space. The radial rows of desks afford a generous space on which to place your books, or your head if you are overwhelmed, and each desk has its own fold-away built into the upright. A truly luxurious place to learn!

20. Bow Street Magistrates' Court

MONDAY 6TH MARCH 2006

I often walk past the crowds of cameras and journalists awaiting media personalities attending Bow Street Magistrates' Court. But today it's quiet, apart from one man who runs out crying 'I'm free, I'm free' – obviously a good day for him! The cheery phone boxes huddled outside, which must have been in constant use only ten years ago, now only have the occasional occupant, but are becoming celebrities in themselves as tourists pose for their snapshot with the design classic British phone box.

21. St James's Park

TUESDAY 16TH MARCH 2006

The sun is out and the wind is raw. I'm feeling a little lost (metaphorically speaking) and wasn't going to sketch, but suddenly out of the corner of my eye, there they were, the beautiful brazen pelicans preening and puffing, one even venturing onto the public footpath, even allowing curious passers-by to stroke his feathers. One of the others continued to flap his wings, as if by sheer will he would overcome his clipped wing and take to the air, but it was not to be. Mr Pelican just flapped down to the water, scaring a few pigeons on the way, and swam to his destination instead, unbeaten, and leaving me a little uplifted.

22. Regent's Canal from Vincent Terrace

WEDNESDAY 22ND AND THURSDAY 23RD MARCH 2006

I have a squirrel behind me happily munching through a salad of crocus flowers, followed by a fruit shortcake biscuit (unknown origin), and various birds making overtures to one another. Yes, spring is tentatively in the air, which must be especially welcome to those who spend a long winter on the narrow boats.

23. Spitalfields

THURSDAY 23RD AND TUESDAY 28TH MARCH 2006

The seductive sunshine of Thursday was spiced up today by hail and rain, but fortunately I'm standing in front of the London Fruit Exchange and the London Wall Exchange which has a deep, well-sheltered entrance, for some protection.

24. Brick Lane

THURSDAY 30TH MARCH 2006

Familiarity and exoticism combine as you wander down Brick Lane – or perhaps more fittingly Banglalane – with rich spicy smells emanating from the windows, and shalwar kameezes and pristine white skull caps outnumbering the suits from a block or two away who come here for lunch.

25. From the top of Monument

FRIDAY 31ST MARCH 2006

The wind greeted me by trying to tear the pages from my sketchbook, but was cunningly foiled by my clothes pegs securing the pages. This fabulous view was the only spot sheltered from the wind racing across the skies.

26. Green Park

THURSDAY APRIL 6TH 2006

After reassuring a policewoman in Green Park that I was indeed painting the daffodils against the lovely backdrop of Queen's Walk, and not counting people going in and out of St James's Palace and Clarence House, amazingly a butterfly, a beautiful terracotta and dark pink one with black spots and unknown identity (as I only know Red Admirals and Tortoiseshells), fluttered down and sat next to me.

27. Arsenal Football Club

SUNDAY 15TH APRIL 2006

This is the view from seat 65, row KK in the North Stand of Arsenal's beloved ground at Highbury – when everyone is sitting down, which is not often, since with any good football match people are up and down from their seats as fast as the ball moves up and down the pitch, and then the view is one of thousands of heads and hands.

28. Covent Garden

THURSDAY APRIL 20TH 2006

This is where expressions such as 'life is a theatre and 'the theatre of life' are made most magnificently manifest. Even Mr Inigo Jones's St Paul's Church juts and struts proudly into the arena, and if you hurry along the sidewings of Henrietta Street or King Street you can go through the passages 'backstage' into the pretty, peaceful and flower-filled churchyard for respite before going on with the show.

29. Tower Bridge

FRIDAY 28TH APRIL AND WEDNESDAY 3RD MAY 2006

Passing by the bustling St Katherine's Docks and Alderman's Stairs, you go through an unpromising passageway which leads out to a large, empty, modern brick terrace. It's a fairly barren place, but, hey, you have this view virtually to yourself, and with the sun out and the wind elsewhere – it is balmy.

30. Highbury Stadium

THURSDAY 4TH MAY AND SUNDAY 7TH MAY 2006

The final salute to a piece of footballing history spanning ninety-three years from 1913 until today. and in true Gunners' style, Arsenal leaves its beloved Highbury home with a real bang, celebrating a 4–2 victory that ensures Champions' League football in the new Emirates Stadium next season. But it is this lovely listed East Stand that has so many stories to tell…

31. The Royal Albert Hall

FRIDAY 5TH MAY AND MONDAY 8TH MAY 2006

The people in their foldaway chairs, who've been queuing all day, are having to use their newspapers as makeshift sun protection. But it's worth the wait, especially for the promenade concerts – a bargain is to be had with a space up in the Gods or down in the arena area, enveloped in world-class music: culture accessible to all.

32. Middle Temple

WEDNESDAY 10TH MAY 2006 AND THURSDAY 11TH MAY 2006

The four Inns of Court are like a tranquil parallel universe from another age, with their stunning gardens, fountains, intersecting courtyards, alleys and ancient buildings. This is some other world!

33. Fleet Street and the Strand

FRIDAY 12TH MAY 2006

Bravely standing in the middle of a very busy Fleet Street, Mr Dragon guards the western city limits, where Fleet Street ends and the Strand begins.

34. Oxford Circus

WEDNESDAY 17TH MAY 2006

Oxford Circus – and what a circus it is! Even early in the morning the crowds and traffic are in full flow, and it's pollution paradise as I keep brushing away these little black flecks that descend from the air onto my sketch. This intersection of Regent Street with Oxford Street is very elegant, if you can find a space (such as this traffic island) to see it before being sucked back into the madness where you are bombarded by fliers, posters, signboards, shop windows, all with the message, shop, shop, shop.

35. Liverpool Street Station

FRIDAY 19TH AND SUNDAY 21ST MAY 2006

It always seems to be packed, but with the elegant 'train station glazed roofs' continuing into the vast entrance hall on the elegant columns, you feel there is still room to breathe.

36. The Savoy

THURSDAY 25TH MAY 2006

I might as well have had a sign above my head saying tourist information, for the amount of directions I have given today. A passer-by stopped to make sure I'd drawn the traffic going into the Savoy forecourt on the right. Apparently it's the only street in the UK where traffic has to do this – a little eccentricity to add to this wonderful entrance.

37. Frith Street

WEDNESDAY 31ST MAY 2006

A wonderful treat, where you almost feel like you're on holiday, is to take a tea or coffee and some yummy pastry and sit outside one of the cafés in Soho on an early sunny morning, and watch the world go by – before it gets really crowded.

38. Fortnum & Masons

FRIDAY 2ND JUNE 2006

Normally, I wouldn't be able to draw this view, since I would be standing in the middle of some exquisite display, but I have found a place by the boarded-off central area, behind which a busy refurbishment is taking place for the tercentenary next year. Service is second nature here: the staff are very helpful and attentive, even to impecunious artists!

39. Westminster Bridge

FRIDAY 15TH AND FRIDAY 22ND FEBRUARY 2002

Parliament is in recess and I had this absolutely incredible view almost all to myself. Now that is a privilege. And sitting in the terrace you get to hear Big Ben twice each time he rings out, as the sonorous sounds bounce across the Thames and echo back in reply.

40. The Houses of Parliament

FRIDAY JUNE 21ST 2002

So today our World Cup dreams are dashed for another four years and there is a general sense of slight sadness in the air. But life goes on and I was amazed sitting here by Westminster Bridge to see a cormorant in the fast-flowing river, diving for two sizeable fish which he had trouble devouring as they writhed about. Poor things…

41. St James's Palace

THURSDAY NOVEMBER 11TH 2004

Armistice Day – I actually began this last week, but as luck would have it a very large removal lorry decided that it was an excellent place to park for the next few hours. Undeterred, however, I returned to finish sketching the front portrait of St James's Palace. Built by Henry VIII, with lots of patching, adding and rebuilding, this eccentric patchwork of façade has a wonderful quirkiness and character.

42. Big Ben

FRIDAY 8TH FEBRUARY 2002

I met a couple of the workmen or craftsmen who did the gold leafing of the pinnacles. They were very friendly, normal guys, but they must have a streak of madness to gild the very top delicacies of the 'pineapple and pinnacles' (I think that's what they said it's called). Absolutely mad – but I guess that must be the ultimate view.

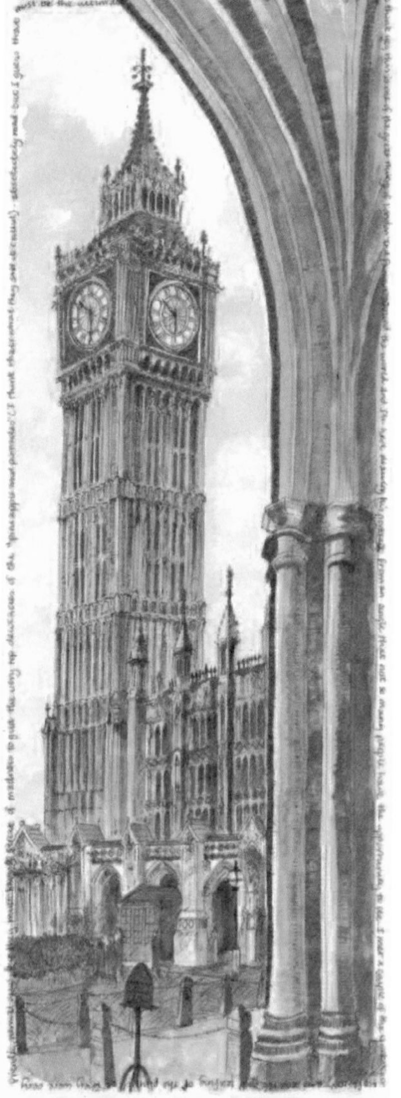

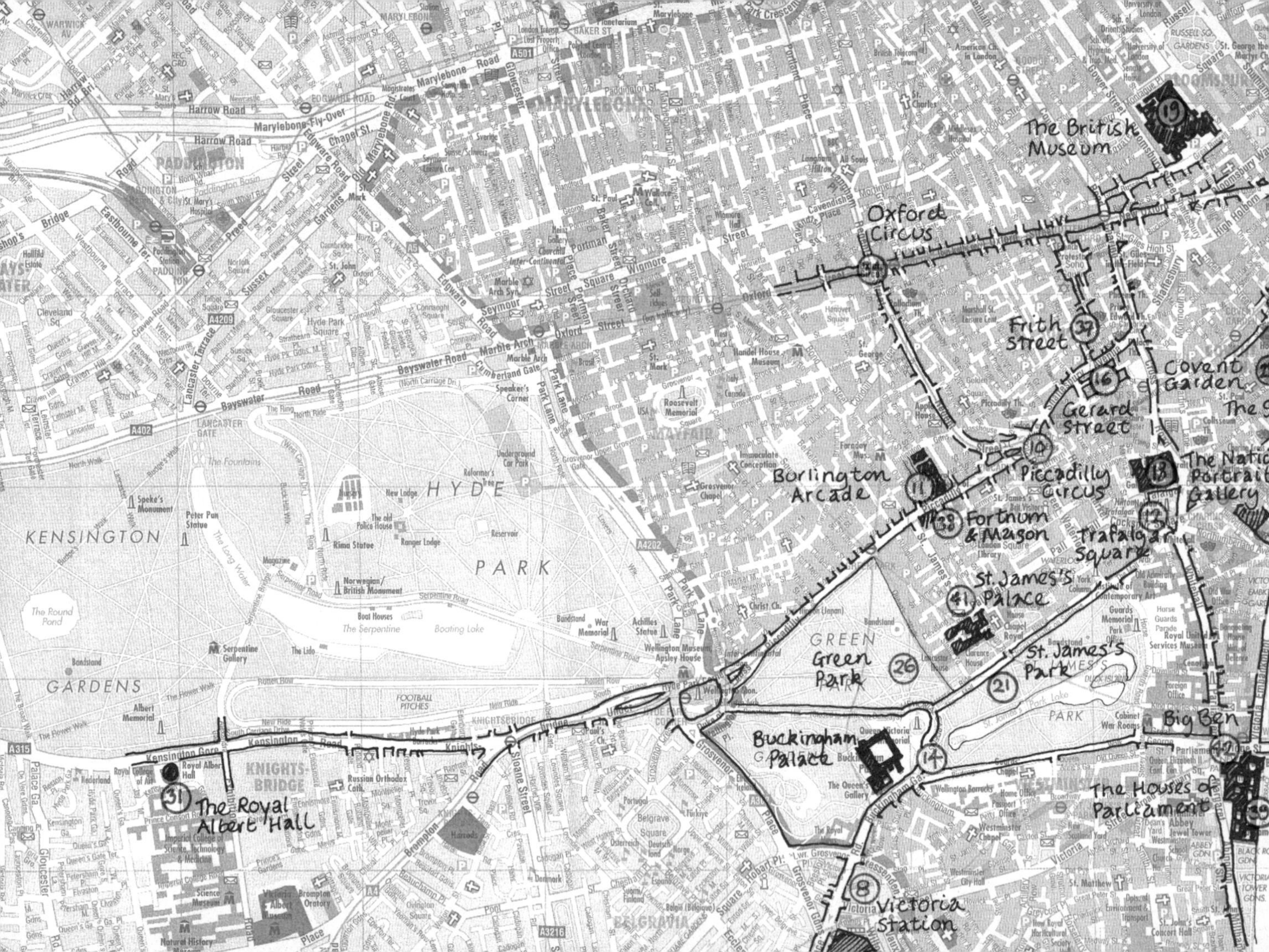
The British Museum
19
Oxford Circus
34
Frith Street
37
16
Covent Garden
Gerard Street
10
Piccadilly Circus
Borlington Arcade
11
38
Fortnum & Mason
18
The National Portrait Gallery
12
Trafalgar Square
41
St. James's Palace
Green Park
26
21
St. James's Park
Big Ben
Buckingham Palace
14
The Houses of Parliament
39
31
The Royal Albert Hall
8
Victoria Station
HYDE
PARK
KENSINGTON
GARDENS
MARYLEBONE
PADDINGTON
MAYFAIR
KNIGHTSBRIDGE
BELGRAVIA
BLOOMSBURY
Marylebone Road
Harrow Road
Bayswater Road
Oxford Street
Park Lane
The Serpentine
The Long Water
The Round Pond